SWEET INSPIRATIONS

"A Cookbook of Fruit Juice Sweetened Desserts"

by

Patti Lynch

Endorsed by
the American Diabetes Association,
Washington Affiliate.

Published by
Sweet Inspirations Inc.

Boehringer Mannheim Corporation, the medical diagnostics company which manufactures Accu-Chek® and Tracer® Blood Glucose Monitors, has selected *Sweet Inspirations* to be part of the HealthLink program for people with diabetes.

BOEHRINGER
MANNHEIM
CORPORATION

Sweet Inspirations Inc.
Suite 2258
1420 N.W. Gilman Blvd.
Issaquah, Washington 98027

Printed in Hong Kong

Seventh Edition — 1994

ISBN 0-9620469-0-6

FOREWORD

When my husband, the great dessert lover of all time, became a diabetic, I discovered that, in order to satisfy his sweet tooth of many years, I was going to have to learn to cook without sugar. No problem, right? Just run down to the nearest book store and purchase a book filled with tasty, sugar-free recipes ... WRONG!

To my amazement, no such book existed. Oh, there were books with synthetic substitutes, but they were impossible recipes to use and less than exciting to eat. My only recourse was to discover my own formulas. Over the next four years, our kitchen became a laboratory and my husband became, you guessed it, a dessert experimenter.

Patti

It's not easy living without sugar in a world where most packaged ingredients contain sugar. And forget restaurants. They are anything but sugar-free! I thought I was never going to taste a scrumptious chocolate cake or a hot delicious fresh baked apple pie again. But, thanks to my wife's diligent and creative efforts, I now enjoy a wide variety of desserts in controlled moderate quantities. And, I am continuing my role as dessert experimenter for our next book.

Ron

NOTE: Anyone with a medical problem such as diabetes should consult a physician with respect to any dietary recipe.

Special thanks ...

To the dearest parents: Ron and Pat Stelzig, and Don O. Lynch, for their loyalty, support, and encouragement in this production.
To the dearest of all Aunts: Vonnie Adams..for letting me laugh, cry, and vent my frustrations!

This book is dedicated to the memory of Audrey Lynch, great cook and great Mother.

TABLE OF CONTENTS

WHY NOT SUGAR?

Are you the type of person who periodically has a craving for something sweet? Do you find yourself sometimes gorging on a sweet roll or a candy bar or even perhaps a whole package of cookies? And then you discover that you're not satisfied?

You have to have more! Without a second thought, you rationalize that "one more bite" won't hurt and before you know it, you've consumed enough calories to sustain you for the next week! In some people, this can produce what is known as a sugar high. You've overdone it, so in order to justify your actions, you make up your mind to stop eating sweets for the next week (well, maybe a day). Now, you begin to have withdrawal pains; sometimes referred to as a sugar low.

You become grumpy and irritable. You kick the cat, scream at the kids, and challenge your loving mate on each and every issue discussed. These responses could be attributed to poor eating habits which generally include large quantities of sugar.

Don't feel alone. There are many who face this situation constantly. In fact, each American consumes an average of 95 lbs. of table sugar yearly and does so without the knowledge that sugar has zero food value. (Some figures range as high as 114 lbs. per person when including products containing sweeteners such as corn syrup.)

A poor diet, high in sugar and/or fat, can aggravate many medical conditions such as: heart disease, anorexia, cancer, and diabetes. Too much sugar can result in uncontrolled blood sugar levels in people who have diabetes or hypoglycemia.

So, in order to alter the situation, we spend millions yearly on diets, health foods, and fitness salons. We start using sugar substitutes and drinking diet sodas. Then we fall victim to advertisers who promise us the body of a star or starlet if we would but use their products. Unfortunately, we discover that it's all a bust. It tastes lousy, costs and arm and a leg, and doesn't satisfy.

Is there an answer to reducing your sugar consumption while continuing to enjoy delicious desserts? Yes, there is! You're reading it!

SWEET INSPIRATIONS is the book just for you! An extreme amount of care has been taken to ensure that every dessert contained in this book is nutritionally valuable, free of commercially processed sugar, free of sugar substitutes, and most tantalizing in flavor. Herein, you will find all of your favorites and the flavors you have always enjoyed without the use of table sugar.

Cakes, cookies, cream pies, ice creams, frostings, and many other tasty categories are represented. And for chocolate lovers, we have included numerous recipes filled with your favorite passion. It is with a great deal of pleasure that this book is presented in order that your sweet tooth may be satisfied and your good health be maintained. It is our sincere desire that you will indeed enjoy discovering your **SWEET INSPIRATIONS!**

THE TRUTH ABOUT SWEETENERS

There are various sugar substitutes on the market which are non-calorie sweeteners. They are usually available in three forms: liquid, granulated, and tablet. Regrettably, these sweeteners never quite successfully substitute for sugar. The granulated product is not useful in cooking; the tablet and liquid can produce an unpleasant or bitter taste if too much is used.

If used, sugar substitutes are usually added toward the end of the cooking procedure in order that the sweetness is not diminished. Most significantly, they never taste quite right under any circumstances.

What's so unique about SWEET INSPIRATIONS?

All of the recipes in SWEET INSPIRATIONS are void of sugar substitutes and raw or refined sugar. Instead, fruit sweeteners have been used because they are made without refined sugar, preservatives, bulk or thickeners, or artificial sweeteners. Fruit sweeteners are nutritionally beneficial and considered a whole food rather than a refined by-product.

They taste nearly twice as sweet as sugar, therefore, one advantage in using them as a sweetening agent is that you only need use about half as much sweetener as you would sugar. In addition, since they metabolize more slowly than sugar, they are less likely to produce a "sugar high" or a "sugar low." Fruit sweeteners, as with fruits or juices, need to be eaten in moderation by persons with diabetes

Although these desserts are sweet and tasty, and a great alternative for those desiring no refined sugar, they should be eaten in a conscientious manner. Below is a list of brands of Fruit Sweeteners, and companies which produce Fruit Sweetened products. These products are available in gourmet, health food, and grocery outlets.

SWEET INSPIRATIONS recipes have been developed using fruit sweetened products.

COMPANIES PRODUCING FRUIT SWEETENED PRODUCTS

AMERICAN SPOON FOODS: 1668 CLARION ST. BOX 566, PETOSKY, MI. 49770. (800) 222 5886. Retail & Mail Order. Fruit Spreads & Toppings./

BARBARA'S BAKERY PRODUCTS: 3900 CYPRESS DR. PETALUMA, CA. 94954. Fudge Topping, cookies, cereals, granola bars.

CAFE GLACE: WALNUT CREEK, CA. Fruit juice sweetened ice cream.

CASCADIAN FARMS: P.O. BOX 568, 311 DILLARD ST. CONCRETE, WA. 98237 (206) 853 8175. Fruit sweetener, organic products.

CHUKAR CHERRIES: PROSSER, WA. 99350. (509) 786 2055. Dried pitted bing cherries.

CLEARBROOK FARMS: 5514 FAIR LANE, FAIRFAX, OHIO 45227 (800) 888 3276. Jams, jellies, spreads.

GLORIA SAMPLE & CO.: 199 EAST AVENUE, LAKE OSWEGO, OREGON 97034. (800) 782 5881. Spreads, sauces, chutneys, marmalades, catsups, vinegars.

GORMLY ORCHARDS: RR 1, BOX 1300, PITTSFORD, VT. 05763. (802) 483 2400. Apple Sweetener (cider syrup), cider jellies, syrups. Retail & Mail Order.

HEALTH VALLEY FOODS: 16100 FOOTHILLS BLVD. IRWINDALE, CA 91706.Fruit juice sweetened cookies, cereals, granola bars.

KOZLOWSKI FARMS: 5566 GRAVENSTEIN HWY. FORESTVILLE, CA 95436. (707) 887 1587. Jams and spreads.

MRS. STEEL'S: 425 E. HECTOR ST. CONSHOHOCKEN, PA 19428. (215) 828 9430 * Fudge & Butterscotch Topping, fruit syrups. *Toppings use Lycasin (a sugar alcohol).

MYSTIC LAKES: 1439 244TH AVE N.E. REDMOND, WA. (206) 868 2029. Fruit Sweetener.

SUNSPIRE: SUNLIGHT FOODS, INC. 2114 ADAMS AVE. SAN LEANDRO, CA 94577. Chocolate chips. (sweetened with barley malt.) Vanilla chips, Peanut butter chips, a variety of delicious candies such as Turtles, English Toffee, Chocolate covered raisins and peanuts.

THOUSAND STARS INC.: P.O. BOX 70, JUNCTION CITY, OREGON 97448 Fruit juice sweetened non fat yogurt.

WAX ORCHARDS: 22744 WAX ORCHARDS RD. SW. VASHON, WA 98070. (800) 634 6132. Fruit Sweetener, (various sizes) Fudge Topping. (five flavors and fat free), preserves, syrups, chutneys. Incredible variety of fruit sweetened products. All products analyzed for Diabetics. Retail and Mail Order.

* GUILTLESS GOURMET: (512) 443 4373. A Great Find! No Oil Tortilla Chips. Fat Free Black bean Dip, and Pinto Bean Dip.

FRUIT SWEETENERS

Because WAX ORCHARDS* produces such high quality products in such variety, we preferred using their products in creating our recipes. WAX ORCHARDS fruit sweetener is Trademarked as FRUIT SWEET*. It is a thick, golden liquid made of concentrated peach and pear juices, and unsweetened pineapple syrup. It tastes 1 1/2 to 2 times sweeter than sugar. This blend is de-acidified, and works well in baking.

FORMULA FOR FRUIT SWEETENER USING JUICE

Below you will find a formula for substituting frozen fruit juice concentrate combined with granulated fructose, in place of liquid fruit sweeteners in the sweet inspirations recipes.Liquid fruit sweetener is considered a humectant, which means that it keeps the moisture in the baked product. The primary difference in using the frozen concentrated juice with granulated fructose is that the end product may be a little drier. For this reason you may want to shorten your baking time slightly.

Formula:

If recipe calls for 1/2 cup fruit sweetener, use 1/2 cup frozen fruit juice concentrate* plus half as much (1/4 cup) granulated fructose.

If recipe calls for 2/3 cup fruit sweetener, use 2/3 cup frozen fruit juice concentrate* plus half as much (1/3 cup) granulated fructose.

* Use an unsweetened bland juice such as apple juice concentrate, or one of the dole products: Orchard peach works well.

MIXING TIP:
When combining the fruit sweetener and margarine for each recipe, microwave these two ingredients together on Medium high for thirty seconds and they will blend perfectly.

TIPS ON FAT:
Fruit sweetener is usually a combination of peach and pear juice concentrate, with a small amount of pineapple syrup. In this form, it is considered a humectant. It keeps the moisture in the baked product, and enables you to eliminate some of the required fat in a recipe. Even in my recipes, as they are written, you may replace half of the oil or margarine called for in a recipe with non-fat yogurt. (Example: if a recipe calls for 1/2 cup of margarine, reduce margarine to 1/4 cup & add 1/4 cup of non fat yogurt.) This does not work in something like pie crust or a crisp rolled cookie, but is great for bars, breads, muffins etc. I also only use the egg whites, leaving out the yolk, and *not* replacing it with an extra white. These two steps will cut the fat grams in half.

If you desire to make a crispie rolled cookie, you may want to replace part of the liquid fruit sweetener with granulated fructose. This may be purchased at any grocery store.
The calories per teaspoon are the same as the fruit sweetener.

COCONUT, EGGS, AND SALT

In the development of the **SWEET INSPIRATIONS** recipes, a concerted effort was made to limit the quantity of food ingredients which are high in sugar and/or high cholesterol fats. Because of this, the authors feel a need to comment on three ingredients which appear in some of the recipes.

Coconut:
Where called for, sweetened coconut was used in place of unsweetened coconut. The fat content is higher in unsweetened coconut and represents more of a dietary problem than the small amount of sugar in sweetened coconut. If coconut is not desired, slivered almonds can be used as a substitute as they contain the lowest amount of fat in the nut family.

Eggs:
Though eggs were used sparingly in the recipes, an egg substitute or two egg whites may be used in place of each egg called for in a recipe, thus eliminating the yolks entirely. If egg whites alone are substituted, they should be beaten before adding them to other ingredients.

Salt:
If necessary, a salt substitute can be used in those recipes requiring salt.

A PERSONAL PERSPECTIVE

There are many benefits derived from not eating sugar. I, personally, cannot leave it alone (once I start eating it). Because sugar is so quickly absorbed into the blood stream, it elevates my blood sugar and gives me high energy for a short time followed by a long-lasting low and a feeling of no energy.

If the cycle continues, it can lead me into a feeling of depression. Fruit sweeteners do not metabolize as quickly as sugar, consequently, a sugar high and subsequent low is minimized. With fruit sweeteners, your "sweet tooth" is satisfied and you are not concentrating on how many chocolate chips are left in the bag.

For me, this has been great, since I have spent years exercising and trying to keep my weight under control. As a small person, this has probably been a greater challenge for me than for most.

Now, I can enjoy a sweet treat without going "bananas", without dreaming of food (don't laugh), without destroying my complexion, or enlarging my thighs! Using fruit sweeteners gives me energy without being "hyper." This is a wonderful way to stay in shape after a weight loss program. And for parents, this is a marvelous solution to the "sugar-high" problem so common with children today. Virtually everyone from sports enthusiasts to health conscious adults and children can benefit from the use of fruit sweeteners as part of a nutritional diet.

I do not use fruit sweeteners as an excuse to over-indulge, but rather as a pleasant addition to a well balanced meal which includes fresh vegetables, lean meat, and complex carbohydrates. Desserts are a special treat after a light dinner or the finale to a holiday meal. Balance, as in all aspects of life, is the key ...

Good eating! Good health! **ENJOY!**

ACKNOWLEDGMENT

I wish to express my thanks and appreciation for the many hours invested in calculating the exchanges on the **SWEET INSPIRATIONS** recipes by **Margaret O'Leary, R.D.,C.D.E.,** clinical dietician, **BENAROYA DIABETES CENTER**, Virginia Mason Medical Center, Seattle WA, specializing in diabetes care and education.

◆

NOTE: Even though the recipes require less fruit sweetener than would be necessary if sugar were used, it is important for people with diet restrictions to take care that the food item is incorporated into an individual meal plan.

NOTES

NOTES

Cookies & Bars

©1989 PK

NOTES

OATMEAL RAISIN COOKIES

Mom always made these great snack cookies!

2/3 cup margarine
3/4 cup fruit sweetener
2 eggs
2 tsp. vanilla
2 cups flour / 1 c. whole wheat
1 tsp. baking soda
1 tsp. salt
2 tsp. cinnamon
1 1/2 cups rolled oats
1/4 cup coconut, shredded (optional)
1/2 cup raisins
1/2 cup nut, chopped (optional)

Cream margarine and fruit sweetener. Mix in eggs, one at a time, until fluffy. Add vanilla. In medium bowl, sift together flour, baking soda, salt, and cinnamon. Add to creamed mixture. Fold in oats, coconut, raisins, nuts. (If desired you may delete coconut and add extra 1/2 cup rolled oats). Drop by teaspoonfuls onto Teflon coated baking sheet. Flatten with fork or bottom of glass. Bake 8-10 minutes at 350 degrees.

Makes 24 cookies.

1 cookie = 1 bread, 1 fat exchanges
135 calories   6 grams fat
18 grams carb.   23 mg sodium
3 grams protein   145 mg cholesterol

Note: If coconut and nuts are added, add 20 calories and 2 grams fat per cookie.

Good. I used cooked down Apple Juice Concentrate, and dough was wet, so added another cup of oatmeal.

1

UN-SUGAR COOKIES

Don't be fooled by the title. These scrumptious
goodies taste just like the "real McCoy"!

> 3/4 cup margarine
> 2/3 cup fruit sweetener
> 2 eggs
> 2 tsp. vanilla
> 2 cups flour
> 1 tsp. baking powder
> 1 tsp. salt

Mix margarine, fruit sweetener thoroughly. Beat
in eggs and vanilla. Combine flour, salt and
baking powder together. Blend in. Chill dough 1
hour. Heat oven to 350. Roll dough 1/8" thick on
lightly floured surface. Cut with round or other
shape cookie cutter. Place on Teflon coated
baking sheet. If desired, brush lightly with
fruit sweetener. Bake 5-7 minutes. Makes about 2
dozen cookies. For holidays, add 2-3 drops food
coloring to fruit sweetener used for glaze.

Makes 24 cookies.

1 cookie = 2/3 bread, 1 fat exchanges
105 calories   6 grams fat
11 grams carb.   153 mg sodium
2 grams protein   22 mg cholesterol

2

CREAM FILLED ALMOND DELIGHTS

You'll love the tasty combination of raspberry and chocolate!

3/4 cup margarine
1/2 cup fruit sweetener
1 egg
1/2 cup ground blanched almonds
2 tsp. almond extract
2 cups flour

Frosting:
1/4 cup raspberries or fruit sweetened raspberry jam or jelly
1/4 cup low-fat Neufchatel
2 Tbsp. fruit sweetener
1/4 cup fruit sweetened fudge sauce

Cream margarine and fruit sweetener. Beat in egg. Add nuts and extract and stir well. Add flour and blend well. Roll dough 1/8" thick on floured board. Cut into cookies with round cutter. Bake on ungreased baking sheet 5 minutes at 350. Cool. Frost with raspberry frosting. Drizzle with melted fudge sauce.

Makes 30 cookies.

1 cookie = 2/3 fruit, 1 fat exchanges
110 calories   6 grams fat
11 grams carb.   63 mg sodium
2 grams protein   10 mg cholesterol

Note: No significant difference in nutrient values using fresh raspberries or fruit sweetened jam - when used in this amount.

GINGER SNAPPERS

Always a favorite with afternoon tea!

 1/2 cup margarine
 2/3 cup fruit sweetener
 1 egg
 1 1/2 cups flour
 1 tsp. baking soda
 1 tsp. cinnamon
 1 tsp. cloves
 1 tsp. ginger

Cream margarine and fruit sweetener. Beat in egg.
In separate bowl, combine the dry ingredients.
Add this mixture to first mixture. Stir in
thoroughly. Roll dough into walnut size balls and
place on prepared baking sheet. Flatten with
fork. Bake 6 minutes at 350. If desired, brush
cookie tops with small amount of fruit sweetener
to glaze.

Makes 24 cookies.

1 cookie = 1/2 bread, 1 fat exchanges
75 calories   4 grams fat
8 grams carb.   80 mg sodium
1 gram protein   11 mg cholesterol

BUNNY'S CHOCOLATE COOKIES

Excellent partner for a cup of hot coffee!

4 Tbsp. cocoa
1 cup margarine
2/3 cup fruit sweetener
3 Tbsp. fruit sweetened fudge sauce
1 Tbsp. vanilla
2 eggs
3 cup flour
1 tsp. salt
2 tsp. baking powder
2/3 cup chopped nuts (optional)
1 cup raisins (optional)

Cream cocoa, margarine, fruit sweetener, and fudge sauce. Beat in eggs and vanilla. Combine dry ingredients in separate bowl, then stir into creamed mixture. Add nuts and raisins.
Drop by teaspoonfuls onto baking sheet which has been sprayed with non-stick coating. Bake 6 minutes at 350 degrees. If desired, drizzle heated fudge sauce over each cookie or frost with CREAM CHEESE FROSTING. (see frostings)

Makes 36 cookies.

1 cookie = 1 bread, 1 fat exchanges
130 calories   7 grams fat
15 grams carb.   135 mg sodium
2 grams protein   15 mg cholesterol

NOTE: nutrient values do not include frosting

CRUNCHIES

Want something different for your party? These will disappear fast!

1/2 cup margarine
2/3 cup fruit sweetener
1 egg
2 tsp. vanilla
1 cup flour
1/2 tsp. baking soda
1/4 tsp. baking powder
1/4 tsp. salt
1 tsp. cinnamon
1 cup oatmeal
1 cup cornflakes (crushed)
1/2 cup coconut (optional)
1/2 cup chopped nuts (optional)

Cream margarine, fruit sweetener. Add egg and vanilla. Combine flour, baking soda, salt, baking powder separately. Add flour mixture to creamed ingredients. Stir in oatmeal and cornflakes. Add nuts and coconut. Roll into 1" balls and place onto Teflon cookie sheet. Bake at 325 degrees for 5-6 minutes.

Makes 36 cookies.

1 cookie = 1/2 bread, 1/2 fat (no coconut, nuts)
60 calories   3 grams fat
7 grams carb.   66 mg sodium
1 gram protein   8 mg cholesterol

Note: If coconut and nuts are included, add 15 calories, 1 gram carb, 1 gram fat

SNACKDOODLES

Like the name says: a great snack treat!

> 2/3 cup margarine
> 2/3 cup fruit sweetener
> 2 eggs
> 2 1/4 cup flour
> 1 1/2 tsp. cream of tartar
> 1 tsp. baking soda
> 1/4 tsp. salt

Mix margarine and fruit sweetener together. Blend in eggs. Beat well. Mix dry ingredients together and add to creamed mixture. Shape dough in 1" balls. Dip each cookie top into mixture of 3 Tbsp. Fruit sweetener and 2 tsp. cinnamon. Place on Teflon coated baking sheet. Bake 6-8 minutes at 350 degrees.

Makes 30 cookies.

1 cookie = 2/3 bread, 1 fat exchanges
90 calories   4 grams fat
10 grams carb.   95 mg sodium
1 gram protein   18 mg cholesterol

OPEN SESAME COOKIES

Ali Baba's favorite!

        2/3 cup fruit sweetener
        2/3 cup margarine
        2 eggs
        1 tsp. vanilla
        2 Tbsp. toasted sesame seeds
        2 1/4 cups flour
        1 tsp. salt
        1/2 tsp. baking powder

Cream fruit sweetener, and margarine thoroughly. Blend in eggs and vanilla. Add sesame seeds. Combine flour, salt, and baking powder separately; then blend into dough. Shape dough into 1" balls. Press hole (thumbprint) in center of each cookie. Place on Teflon coated cookie sheet. Bake 6-8 minutes at 350. Cool. Fill thumbprint of each cookie with 1 teaspoonful fudge sauce filling: (combine 1/4 cup fudge sauce and 1 tsp. orange flavoring or Grand Marnier and 1 tbsp. grated orange rind).

Makes 2 dozen.

1 cookie = 1 bread, 1 fat exchanges
115 calories   6 grams fat
13 grams carb.   155 mg sodium
2 grams protein   22 mg cholesterol

SHORT CAKES

Adapted from an old English recipe. Excellent with tea!

    1 cup margarine
    2/3 cup fruit sweetener — *or ½ c. Sucanat*
    1 cup flour   *(or a little less)*
    1 cup rice flour

Cream margarine and fruit sweetener thoroughly.
Measure flour, then sift into creamed mixture.
Roll dough out on floured surface (1/4" thick).
Cut into rounds or fancy shapes. Bake at 350
degrees for 10 minutes or until light golden
brown. Cool.

Makes 24 cookies.

1 cookie = 1 bread, 1 fat exchanges
125 calories	8 grams fat
13 grams carb.	90 mg sodium
1 gram protein	0 mg cholesterol

This doesn't work in my shortbread Mold. It really sticks.

9

FARM HOUSE COOKIES

Try these with a glass of ice-cold milk!

    3/4 cup shortening
    3/4 cup fruit sweetener
    2 eggs
    1 cup buttermilk
    1 tsp. vanilla
    1/2 tsp. baking soda
    2 tsp. baking powder
    1/2 tsp. nutmeg
    1/2 tsp. salt
    3 1/4 cups flour

Cream shortening and fruit sweetener. Beat in eggs, one at a time. Add buttermilk and vanilla. Combine all dry ingredients and add slowly to creamed mixture. Refrigerate dough for one hour. Roll dough out 1/4" thick on floured board. Cut with large round cutter (3"). Place cookies onto Teflon baking sheet one inch apart. Place 3 raisins in center of each cookie (optional). Bake at 350 for 8 - 10 minutes.

Makes 36 cookies.

1 cookie = 2/3 bread, 1 fat exchanges
95 calories   4 grams fat
12 grams carb.   112 mg sodium
2 grams protein   16 mg cholesterol

GINGER SWEETS

Good on a cold morning with a cup of hot coffee!

 1/2 cup margarine
 1/2 cup fruit sweetener
 1 egg
 1/2 tsp. vanilla
 1 cup flour
 1/2 tsp. baking soda
 1/4 tsp. salt
 2 tsp. ginger
 1/2 cup chopped walnuts (optional)

In large bowl, cream together first four ingredients. Beat 3 minutes. Combine dry ingredients separately and add slowly to beaten mixture, continuing to beat. Stir in nuts. On baking sheet, which has been coated with non-stick spray, drop cookies by spoonfuls about 2" apart. Bake at 350 degrees for 8 minutes. Remove from sheet with metal spatula.

Makes 24 cookies.

1 cookie = 1/2 bread, 1 fat exchanges
85 calories   6 grams fat
7 grams carb.   85 mg sodium
2 grams protein   11 mg cholesterol

CHOCOLATE CHIP COOKIES

These are an all-time favorite with the kids!

1 cup margarine
3/4 cup fruit sweetener
2 eggs
1 tsp. vanilla
2 cup flour
1 tsp. baking soda
1/2 tsp. salt
1/2 tsp. baking powder
1 cup chocolate chips sweetened with
barley malt (unsweetened carob chips may be used)
2 cups rolled oats
1/2 cup chopped nuts (optional)

Blend margarine and fruit sweetener. Add eggs and vanilla and mix well. Combine dry ingredients separately and add to creamed mixture. Stir in chips and oats. Drop by teaspoonful onto Teflon cookie sheet. Bake 6-8 minutes at 350 degrees. For crispie cookies, flatten each cookie with the bottom of a glass or with a fork.

Makes 42 cookies.

1 cookie = 1 bread, 1 fat exchanges
110 calories   6 grams fat
13 grams carb.   106 mg sodium
2 grams protein   13 mg cholesterol

Note: Add 10 calories, 1 gram of fat
if nuts are included.

PEANUT BUTTER COOKIES

An excellent addition to the kid's school lunch!

        1/2 cup margarine
        1/2 cup peanut butter
        1/2 cup fruit sweetener
        1 egg
        1 1/4 cup flour
        1/2 tsp. baking powder
        1/2 tsp. baking soda
        1/4 tsp. salt

Mix margarine, peanut butter, and fruit sweetener. Add egg and blend well. Mix dry ingredients together and blend into creamed mixture. Roll dough into walnut size balls. Place on Teflon coated cookie sheet. Flatten with fork. Bake 7-9 minutes at 350 degrees.

Makes 2 dozen cookies.

1 cookie = 1/2 bread, 1 1/2 fat exchanges
105 calories   7 grams fat
9 grams carb.   116 mg sodium
2 grams protein   11 mg cholesterol

Peanut Butter Chocolate Kisses

Follow above recipe. Roll dough into walnut size balls. Press thumb in center of each cookie. Bake as above. When cool, fill thumbprint with 1/2 tsp. of fruit sweetened fudge sauce.

Note: Addition of 1/2 tsp. fruit sweetened fudge sauce per cookie adds 8 calories and 2 grams of carbohydrate

ONA ONA COOKIES

These are a different and unique treat for your guests!

    1/2 cup margarine
    1/4 cup fruit sweetener
    1/2 cup fruit sweetened fudge topping
    or a fruit sweetened fudge sauce
    2 Tbsp. cocoa
    2 eggs
    2 tsp. vanilla
    1 1/2 cup flour
    1/2 tsp. salt
    1 tsp. baking soda
FILLING:
    1/2 cup peanut butter
    2 Tbsp. fruit sweetener
    1 Tbsp. instant mashed potato flakes

Cream margarine, fruit sweetener and fudge sauce.
Blend in cocoa. Add eggs and vanilla. Mix well.
Separately, combine dry ingredients and add to
creamed mixture. Roll dough into 1" balls. Make
thumbprint dent in center and place on prepared
cookie sheet.

Combine filling ingredients. Fill cavity of each
cookie with 1 tsp. of filling. Bake at 325
degrees for 6 minutes.

Makes 24 cookies.

1 cookie = 1 bread, 1 fat exchanges
127 calories   7 grams fat
13 grams carb.   150 mg sodium
3 grams protein   23 mg cholesterol

HARLEQUINN COOKIES

Taken from a turn-of-the-century recipe, these are quite tasty and colorful!

> 3/4 cup margarine
> 2/3 cup fruit sweetener
> 2 tsp. vanilla
> 1 1/2 cup flour
> 1 tsp. salt
> 1 cup rolled oats

Cream margarine and fruit sweetener. Add vanilla, flour, and salt. Thoroughly mix in oats. Roll into 1" balls. Place on ungreased cookie sheet. Bake 6-8 minutes at 350 degrees. Cool. In saucepan, heat 1/3 cup fruit sweetened fudge sauce. Dip top of each cookie in warmed fudge sauce. Sprinkle cookie tops with chopped nuts.

Makes 24 cookies.

1 cookie = 1 bread, 1 1/2 fat exchanges
140 calories   7 grams fat
17 grams carb.   150 mg sodium
3 grams protein   0 mg cholesterol

Note: Fudge sauce and nuts for topping included in nutrient values.

COWBOY COOKIES

This is how the West was really won!

> 1/2 cup margarine
> 1/2 cup peanut butter
> 2/3 cup fruit sweetener
> 2 eggs
> 1 tsp. vanilla
> 1 1/4 cup flour
> 1 tsp. baking soda
> 1 tsp. salt
> 1 cup rolled oats
> 1/2 cup coconut (optional)
> 1/2 cup raisins (optional)
> 1/2 cup chocolate chips sweetened with
> barley malt.(or unsweetened carob chips)
> 1/2 cup chopped nuts (optional)

Cream margarine, peanut butter, fruit sweetener.
Add eggs and vanilla. Stir well. Combine flour,
salt, and baking soda together then add to
creamed mixture. Fold in oats, coconut, raisins,
chips, and chopped nuts. Drop by teaspoonfuls
onto Teflon baking sheet. Bake at 350 degrees for
6-8 minutes.

Makes 30 cookies.

1 cookie = 2/3 bread, 1 fat exchanges
115 calories   6 grams fat
12 grams carb.   154 mg sodium
3 grams protein   18 mg cholesterol

Note: If optional raisins, nuts, and coconut are
included, add 25 calories, 3 grams carb. and 2 grams
fat per cookie.

CHARLIE BROWN BOYS

The kids will love you for these tasty guys!

    1/2 cup margarine
    2/3 cup fruit sweetener
    1/4 cup water
    2 tsp. rum flavoring
    2 1/2 cup flour
    1 tsp. salt
    1 tsp. baking soda
    3 tsp. ginger
    1 tsp. cloves
    1/2 tsp. nutmeg
    1/2 tsp. allspice

Cream margarine and fruit sweetener. Add water and rum flavoring. Combine dry ingredients and add to creamed mixture slowly, stirring well. Chill dough one hour. On floured surface, roll dough 1/4" thick. Cut with 3" cutter or ginger boy cutter. Bake on Teflon coated sheet at 350 degrees for 6-8 minutes.

Makes 30 cookies.

1 cookie = 1/2 bread, 1 fat exchanges
80 calories   3 grams fat
11 grams carb.   130 mg sodium
1 gram protein   0 mg cholesterol

SANDY BEACH COOKIES

Light and quick to fix. Great for lunches!

> 3/4 cup margarine
> 1/2 cup fruit sweetener
> dash salt
> 1 tsp. vanilla
> 2 cup flour
> 1/2 cup finely chopped nuts (optional)

Blend margarine and fruit sweetener. Add salt and vanilla. Cut in flour. Blend thoroughly. Add nuts. Roll into 1" balls. Place on Teflon coated cookie sheet. Flatten cookies with fork. Bake 6-8 minutes at 350 degrees.

Makes 24 cookies.

1 cookie = 1 bread, 1 fat exchanges
115 calories	7 grams fat
11 grams carb.	66 mg sodium
2 grams protein	0 mg cholesterol

PEANUT BUTTER BON BONS

For the peanut butter lover in your house who just happens to love chocolate also!

1/2 cup fruit sweetener
1/2 cup melted margarine
2/3 cup peanut butter
1/2 cup chopped nuts (optional)
2 cups graham cracker crumbs
TOPPING:
1/2 cup fruit sweetened fudge sauce

Cream together fruit sweetener, margarine, and peanut butter. Stir in nuts and graham cracker crumbs. Roll into 1" balls. Place on cookie sheet and chill one hour. In saucepan, heat 1/2 cup fruit sweetened fudge sauce. Dip top of each cookie into fudge sauce, then cool.

Makes 32 cookies.

1 cookie = 1/2 bread, 1 fat exchanges
95 calories   6 grams fat
9 grams carb.   78 mg sodium
2 grams protein   0 mg cholesterol

Note: If nuts are included, add 10 calories and 1 gram fat

CHOCOLATE CRACKLES

Brighten up your parties with these chocolate delights!

> 1/2 cup vegetable oil
> 4 Tbsp. cocoa
> 3/4 cup fruit sweetener
> 1 eggs + 2 egg whites
> 2 tsp. vanilla
> 1 3/4 cup flour
> 1 1/2 tsp. baking powder
> 1/2 tsp. salt

TOPPING:
> 1/2 cup instant mashed potato flakes
> 3 Tbsp. fruit sweetener

Mix oil, cocoa and fruit sweetener. Blend in egg and egg white. Add vanilla. In separate bowl mix dry ingredients. Add dry ingredients to batter. Drop spoonfuls of dough in topping mixture and roll into walnut size balls. Place cookies on Teflon cookie sheet. Bake 5-8 minutes at 350 degrees.

Makes 24 cookies.

1 cookie = 1 bread, 1 fat exchanges

110 calories	5 grams fat
14 grams carb.	70 mg sodium
2 grams protein	11 mg cholesterol

APRICOT CURLS

A fruity, chewy, delight for your guests!

FILLING:
>   6 oz. dried apricots, chopped
>   1/2 cup fruit sweetener
>   1/3 cup water
>   1 tsp. vanilla

PASTRY:
>   1/2 cup low-fat ricotta cheese, or
>   low-fat Neufchatel cheese
>   1/4 cup margarine
>   1 1/4 cup flour

Combine apricots, sweetener, and water in sauce pan and cook until thickened. Remove from heat and stir in vanilla. Cool.

Blend cheese, margarine, and flour to crumb like consistency. Add a few drops of cold water and roll into a ball. Roll pastry out on a floured surface to a 15" x 18" rectangle. Cut into 3" squares (30 squares). Drop a teaspoonful of filling onto each square. Fold squares into triangles and pinch edges. Place on Teflon coated cookie sheet. Bake 12-15 minutes at 350 degrees.

Makes 30 cookies.

1 cookie = 1 fruit exchange
62 calories	2 grams fat
10 grams carb.	25 mg sodium
1 grams protein	1 mg cholesterol

DATE FILLED COOKIES

Especially good with tea on sunny Spring days!

    2 cups finely chopped dates
    3/4 cup water
    1/3 cup fruit sweetener
    2/3 cup fruit sweetener
    2/3 cup margarine, melted
    2 cups flour
    1 tsp. cream of tartar
    1 tsp. baking soda
    1 tsp. salt
    1 Tbsp. hot water
    1 tsp. vanilla
    1 cup rolled oats

Combine first three ingredients in saucepan. Cook over medium heat, stirring until thickened. Remove from heat and cool thoroughly. In large bowl combine 2/3 cup fruit sweetener and margarine. In separate bowl combine remaining ingredients. Mix well and add to creamed mixture. Stir in rolled oats. Chill dough 1 hour. Roll our 1/8" thick. Cut dough into round cookies with cookie cutter. Place teaspoon of date mixture on each round cookie and top with another cookie. Pinch or flute cookie edges. Bake 8-10 minutes at 350 degrees on Teflon coated cookie sheet.

Makes 36 cookies.

1 cookie = 1 fruit, 1 fat exchanges
110 calories   6 grams fat
18 grams carb.   116 mg sodium
1 grams protein   0 mg cholesterol

MERINGUE KISSES

Soft and quite festive for any occasion!

  3 egg whites
  1 tsp. cornstarch
  1 tsp. cream of tartar
  2 tsp. vanilla
  3 Tbsp. fruit sweetener
  1 cup chocolate chips sweetened with barley
     malt or carob chips
  1/2 cup chopped walnuts (optional)

Beat egg whites until fluffy. Add cornstarch and
cream of tarter. Beat until stiff. Add vanilla.
Slowly add fruit sweetener. Fold in chips and
nuts. Drop by spoonfuls onto foil covered cookie
sheet. Bake 30 minutes at 275 degrees. Cool
thoroughly. For a Christmas cookie: add 1/4 tsp.
peppermint extract and 2-3 drops green food
coloring; delete vanilla.

Makes 30 cookies.

1 cookie = 1/2 fruit, 1/2 fat exchanges
45 calories   2 grams fat
6 grams carb.   7 mg sodium
1 gram protein   0 mg cholesterol

CHOCOLATE CRISPS

Guaranteed to satisfy your chocolate desires!

> 3 egg whites
> 1/4 tsp. cream of tartar
> dash of salt
> 1/4 cup fruit sweetener
> 1 tsp. vanilla
> 1/4 cup fruit sweetened fudge sauce
> 1/2 cup shredded coconut (optional)
> 2 cup rice krispie type cereal
> 1/2 cup mashed potato flakes

Beat egg whites until frothy. Add cream of tartar, salt. Slowly, add fruit sweetener and vanilla. Beat until stiff. Heat fudge sauce slightly; then fold fudge sauce gently into egg white mixture. Fold in coconut, rice cereal, and potato flakes. Drop by teaspoonfuls onto baking sheet which had been covered with ungreased brown paper. Bake at 275 degrees for 30-40 minutes.

Makes 24 cookies.

1 cookie = 1/2 fruit exchange
30 calories	0 grams fat
6 grams carb.	43 mg sodium
1 gram protein	0 mg cholesterol

Note: Addition of coconut adds 10 calories and 1 gram fat per cookie.

MACAROONIES

As American as "Old Glory"; these are a favorite
with the kids!

> 3 egg whites
> 1/4 tsp. cream of tartar
> dash of salt
> 1/4 cup fruit sweetener
> 1/2 tsp. vanilla
> 1 1/2 cup shredded coconut
> 1/4 cup mashed potato flakes

Beat egg whites until frothy. Add cream of tartar
and salt. Slowly, in fine stream, add fruit
sweetener and vanilla. Beat until stiff. Fold in
coconut and potato flakes. Drop by spoonfuls onto
baking sheet covered with ungreased brown paper.
Bake at 275 degrees for 30-40 minutes. Cool
thoroughly before removing from brown paper.

Makes 24 cookies.

3 cookies = 1 bread, 1 fat exchanges
120 calories   6 grams fat
15 grams carb.   190 mg sodium
3 grams protein   0 mg cholesterol

CORNFLAKE MACAROONS

A traditional treat that's a must for coconut lovers!

> 3 egg whites
> 1/4 cup fruit sweetener
> 1 tsp. vanilla
> 1/2 cup shredded coconut
> 1/2 cup chopped nuts
> dash salt
> 3 cup cornflakes

Beat egg whites until stiff. Slowly, in fine stream, add fruit sweetener. Beat one more minute. Fold in all other ingredients in order. Form 24 small clusters on greased baking sheet leaving 1" between cookies. Bake at 275 degrees for 30 minutes. Cool. For Christmas time: 3-4 drops of green or red food coloring can be added with vanilla.

Makes 24 cookies.

3 cookies = 1 bread, 1 fat exchanges
135 calories   6 grams fat
8 grams carb.   136 mg sodium
3 grams protein   0 mg cholesterol

TASSELS

Tiny, individual desserts with pleasure included in every bite!

1/4 cup low-fat Neufchatel
1/3 cup margarine
1 cup flour
1/2 cup fruit sweetener
1 Tbsp. margarine
2 tsp. vanilla
dash salt
1 egg
1 cup walnuts, chopped

Blend Neufchatel, margarine, and flour. Divide dough into 24 walnut sized balls. Press into miniature muffin tin or tiny tart pans. In separate bowl, combine fruit sweetener, margarine and vanilla. Beat in salt and egg. Fold in nuts. Pour small amount of nut mixture into each tart shell. Bake 12-15 minutes at 375 degrees.

Makes 24 cookies.

1 cookie = 1/2 bread, 1 1/2 fat exchanges
100 calories   7 grams fat
8 grams carb.   47 mg sodium
2 grams protein   13 mg cholesterol

ALL TIME BROWNIES

Simply wonderful!

1/2 cup margarine
4 Tbsp. cocoa
1/2 cup fruit sweetener
2 eggs
2/3 cup flour
1 tsp. baking powder
1/4 tsp. salt
1/2 cup chopped nuts (optional)

Blend margarine, cocoa, fruit sweetener. Add eggs, one at a time, beating well after each addition. Mix dry ingredients together separately. Add to chocolate mixture. Fold in nuts. Pour into 9" x 9" pan which has been sprayed with non-stick coating spray. Bake 15-20 minutes at 325 degrees. (Brownie is done if it springs back when lightly touched in center)

Makes 16 brownies.

1 brownie = 2/3 bread, 2 fat exchanges
140 calories   10 grams fat
9 grams carb.   177 mg sodium
2 grams protein   34 mg cholesterol

STICKY CHEWY CHOCOLATE BROWNIES

One of my "decadent" recipes! I love these! Very rich!

> 4 Tbsp. cocoa
> 1/2 cup margarine
> 2/3 cup fruit sweetener
> 2 eggs
> 1 cup flour
> 1 tsp. baking powder
> 1/2 tsp. salt

TOPPING:

> 1/2 cup fruit sweetened fudge sauce
> 1/2 cup chopped nuts (optional)
> 1 tsp. vanilla
> 1 tsp. almond flavoring

Combine cocoa, margarine and fruit sweetener. Add eggs and blend well. Combine dry ingredients and stir into chocolate mixture. Pour into 9" x 9" baking pan which has been sprayed with non-stick coating. In small bowl, mix 1/2 cup fudge sauce with 1/2 cup chopped nuts, 1 tsp. vanilla, and 1 tsp. almond flavoring. Drop teaspoonfuls of the mixture over brownie dough. Bake 12-15 minutes at 350 degrees.

Makes 20 (2") brownies.

1 brownie = 1 bread, 1 fat exchanges
130 calories   7 grams fat
14 grams carb.   125 mg sodium
2 grams protein   27 mg cholesterol

CHOCO-TOFFEE BARS

Rich and soon to be famous!

> 3/4 cup margarine
> 1/2 cup fruit sweetener
> 1 egg
> 1 tsp. vanilla
> 1 3/4 cup flour
> dash salt
> 2/3 cup fruit sweetened fudge sauce

Cream margarine and fruit sweetener. Beat in egg. Blend in vanilla. Add flour and salt. Spread in 9" x 13" oblong pan which has been sprayed with non-stick coating. Bake 15 minutes at 325 degrees. While still warm, spread with fudge sauce. Sprinkle with chopped nuts.

Makes 36 bars.

1 bar = 2/3 bread, 1 fat exchanges
90 calories   5 grams fat
10 grams carb.   60 mg sodium
1 grams protein   8 mg cholesterol

NEW ORLEANS CHOCOLATE SQUARES

A spicy chocolate treat!

> 2/3 cup margarine
> 4 Tbsp. cocoa
> 2/3 cup fruit sweetener
> 2 eggs
> 3/4 cup flour
> 1 tsp. baking powder
> dash salt
> 2 tsp. cinnamon
> 1/4 tsp. cloves
> 2 tsp. vanilla
> 1/2 cup chopped nuts (optional)

Melt together margarine and cocoa. Stir in fruit sweetener until well blended. Beat in eggs. Blend well. Combine dry ingredients separately and add to chocolate mixture. Add vanilla and nuts. Pour into 9" x 9" pan which has been sprayed with non-stick coating. Bake 12 minutes at 325 degrees. (or until firm in center)

Makes 16 squares.

1 square = 2/3 bread, 2 fat exchanges
150 calories	10 grams fat
11 grams carb.	130 mg sodium
2 grams protein	34 mg cholesterol

COCONUT ALMOND SQUARES

Moist and chewy!

    1/2 cup margarine
    1/4 cup fruit sweetener
    1 tsp. vanilla
    1 cup flour
    2 eggs (beaten well)
    1/2 cup fruit sweetener
    1 tsp. vanilla
    1 tsp. rum flavoring
    2 Tbsp. flour
    1/2 tsp. baking powder
    1/2 tsp. salt
    1 cup shredded coconut
    1 cup chopped toasted almonds

Blend first four ingredients. Press into 9" x 13" cake pan as crust. Beat eggs well and add fruit sweetener, vanilla, and rum flavoring. Add flour, baking powder, and salt and mix well. Stir in coconut and nuts. Pour over crust. Bake 25 minutes (or until golden) at 350 degrees. Cool. Cut into squares. Dried fruit, such as apricot bits may be added with coconut for a festive touch.

Makes 36 bars.

1 bar = 1/2 bread, 1 fat exchanges
90 calories   6 grams fat
8 grams carb.   73 mg sodium
2 grams protein   15 mg cholesterol

NUT CRACKER SWEETS

You'll have everyone dancing with delight over
these crunchy critters!

    2 Tbsp. cocoa
    1/2 cup margarine
    1/3 cup fruit sweetener
    1/4 cup fruit sweetened fudge sauce
    dash salt
    1 egg
    2/3 cup graham cracker crumbs (10 squares)
    1/4 cup shredded coconut
    1/3 cup chopped nuts

Heat cocoa and margarine until melted. Add fruit
sweetener and fudge sauce. Mix well. Blend in
salt and egg. Stir in graham cracker crumbs,
coconut, and chopped nuts. Pour into 8" x 8"
square pan which has been sprayed with non-stick
coating. Bake 15-20 minutes at 350 degrees.

Serves 16.

1 serving = 1/2 bread, 1 1/2 fat exchanges
120 calories   8 grams fat
9 grams carb.   105 mg sodium
1 gram protein   17 mg cholesterol

PEANUT BUTTER BARS

Serve this to the ones who love P.B. and J.

1/2 cup margarine
2/3 cup fruit sweetener
1/2 cup peanut butter
1 egg
2 tsp. vanilla
1 cup flour
1/2 tsp. baking soda
1/4 tsp. salt
1 cup oatmeal
1/3 cup fruit sweetened fudge sauce

Topping:
1/4 cup peanut butter
2 Tbsp. fruit sweetener
1 Tbsp. milk

Cream margarine, fruit sweetener, and peanut butter. Beat in egg and vanilla. Separately, combine flour, salt and baking soda. Beat into mixture. Stir in oatmeal. Pour batter into lightly greased 9" x 13" pan. Bake 20-25 minutes at 350 degrees. While bars are still warm, spread with fudge sauce. Combine peanut butter, fruit sweetener and milk. Drizzle over bars and cut into 2" squares.

Makes 36 bars.

1 bar = 1/2 bread, 1 fat exchanges
98 calories   6 grams fat
10 grams carb.   81 mg sodium
2 grams protein   8 mg cholesterol

BLONDIE BROWNIES

Attractive and delicious. Everyone's favorite!

2/3 cup margarine
2/3 cup fruit sweetener
2 eggs
2 tsp. vanilla
1 cup flour
1 tsp. baking soda
1 tsp. salt
1 cup rolled oats
1/2 cup fruit sweetened fudge sauce or 1 cup chocolate chips sweetened with barley malt
1/2 cup chopped nuts (optional)

Combine margarine and fruit sweetener. Beat in eggs, one at a time. Add vanilla. Combine separately: flour, baking soda, and salt and mix into batter. Fold in oats. Spread batter in 9" x 13" cake pan which has been sprayed with non-stick coating. Sprinkle nuts evenly over top. Drop tiny spoonfuls of fudge sauce over entire batter (If using chocolate chips, sprinkle over entire batter). Bake 20-30 minutes at 350 degrees.

Makes 36 brownies.

1 brownie = 1/2 bread, 1 fat exchanges
77 calories   4 grams fat
9 grams carb.   120 mg sodium
1 gram protein   15 mg cholesterol

Note: If nuts are added, increase calories by 10 and fat by 1 gram. If chocolate chips are used in place of fruit sweetened fudge topping:

1 brownie = 1 bread, 1 fat exchanges
98 calories   6 grams fat
11 grams carb.   120 mg sodium
2 gram protein   15 mg cholesterol

FUDGE RIBBON

These are so good, they won't last long. They freeze well, so tuck a few away!

> 3/4 cup margarine
> 3/4 cup fruit sweetener
> 2 eggs
> 2 tsp. vanilla
> 2 cup flour
> 1 tsp. baking soda
> 1 tsp. salt
> 3 cup rolled oats
> 3/4 cup chopped nuts
> 2/3 cup fruit sweetened fudge sauce
> 2 Tbsp. skim milk

Cream margarine and fruit sweetener. Beat in eggs and vanilla. Separately, combine flour, baking soda, and salt. Add dry mixture to dough. Stir in rolled oats and nuts. Press half of dough into 9" x 13" pan which has been sprayed with non-stick coating. Combine fudge sauce and milk and spread over dough. Sprinkle remaining dough as crumbly mixture on top of fudge sauce layer. Bake 20 minutes at 350 degrees. Cut in squares.

Makes 36 squares.

1 square = 1 bread, 1 fat exchanges
132 calories	6 grams fat
16 grams carb.	125 mg sodium
3 grams protein	15 mg cholesterol

TIERED BROWNIES

Each layer is a scrumptious delight!

    1/2 cup flour
    1/4 tsp. baking soda
    1/4 tsp. salt
    1 cup rolled oats
    1/3 cup margarine, melted
    3 Tbsp. fruit sweetener
    1 recipe of ALL TIME BROWNIE dough
    1/4 cup fruit sweetened fudge sauce

Combine flour, baking soda, and salt. Blend well.
Stir in rolled oats, margarine, and fruit
sweetener. Pat mixture into bottom of 9" square
pan, which has been sprayed with a non-stick
coating. Bake 5 minutes at 350 degrees. Mix ALL
TIME BROWNIE dough and spread over baked crust.
Bake an additional 15-20 minutes at 350 degrees.
Remove from oven. While brownies are still warm,
frost with 1/4 cup fudge sauce. Sprinkle with
small amount of chopped nuts, if desired.

Makes 16 brownies.

1 brownie = 1 bread, 3 fat exchanges
200 calories   13 grams fat
18 grams carb.   246 mg sodium
4 grams protein   34 mg cholesterol

CREAM CHEESE BROWNIES

Following ALL TIME BROWNIES recipe, and after pouring batter into 9" x 9" pan, prepare filling.

FILLING:
> 1/4 cup light cream cheese, softened
> 5 teaspoons granulated fructose
> 1 egg white
> 1/4 cup chocolate chips sweetened
> with barley malt

Combine cream cheese, egg white and frutose. Beat well. Stir in chips. Drop spoonfuls on chocolate batter and marble with knife. Bake 10-12 minutes at 325 degrees. While warm, spread with fudge sauce.

Makes 16 brownies.

1 brownie = 1 bread, 2 fat exchanges
180 calories   12 grams fat
14 grams carb.   186 mg sodium
4 grams protein   35 mg cholesterol

CHOCOLATE CARAMEL BARS

A rich gooey Christmas cookie that really is festive!

CRUST:
    1/2 cup margarine or butter
    1/2 cup fruit sweetener
    2 cups flour
    dash salt
FILLING:
    1 Tbsp. cornstarch
    3 Tbsp. water
    1/2 cup evaporated skim milk
    1/2 cup fruit sweetener
    2 tsp. vanilla
TOPPING:
    1/2 cup fruit sweetened fudge sauce
    1/3 cup chopped toasted almonds

Beat butter and fruit sweetener. Add flour and salt.
Mix well. Spray 9" x 13" pan with non-stick coating
spray. Bake until golden, 12-15 min. at 350 degrees. Cool.

In saucepan dissolve cornstarch in water. Add
milk and fruit sweetener. Stir constantly over
medium heat until mixture thickens and bubbles.
Remove from heat and add 2 tsp. vanilla. Cool
slightly and pour over cooked crust. Refrigerate
30 minutes.

Heat fudge sauce. Pour over cooled filling. Gently
spread,then cover with chopped toasted almonds.

Makes 36 bars.

1 bar = 1/2 bread, 1/2 fruit, 1/2 fat exchanges
86 calories   3 grams fat
12 grams carb.   39 mg sodium
1 grams protein   0 mg cholesterol

GEORGIE PORGIE CHERRY CHOCOLATE BARS

Well worth the effort!

    1 tsp. salt
    1/3 cup cornstarch
    5 Tbsp. cocoa
    2 cups skim milk
    2/3 cup fruit sweetener
    3 Tbsp. margarine
    1 16 oz can pie cherries
        canned in water, well drained
        or unsweetened juice
    1 1/2 cups flour
    1 tsp. baking powder
    dash salt
    1 egg, well beaten
    2 Tbsp. vanilla
    1/4 cup fruit sweetened fudge sauce

Combine salt, cornstarch, cocoa, and 1/2 cup milk
in saucepan. Blend until smooth. Add remaining
milk and fruit sweetener. Stir constantly over
medium heat until mixture thickens and begins to
boil. Remove from heat and stir in margarine and
cherries. Set aside. In separate bowl, blend
flour, baking powder, and salt. Stir in pudding.
Add egg and vanilla. Pour entire mixture into a
9x9 inch pan which has been sprayed with
non-stick coating. Bake 25-30 minutes at 350
degrees. While warm, spread with 1/4 cup fruit
sweetened fudge sauce, if desired.

Makes 36 bars.

1 bar = 1 fruit exchange
60 calories   1 grams fat
11 grams carb.   90 mg sodium
1 grams protein   8 mg cholesterol

LUSH LEMON BARS

If you like lemon, these are for you. Tart and tasty! Thank you Kathleen Boyle, of Pastimes!

1 1/2 cup flour
1/2 cup margarine
3 Tbsp. fruit sweetener
1/2 cup shredded coconut
1/2 cup chopped nuts
2/3 cup fruit sweetener
1/3 cup lemon juice
2 eggs + 1 egg white
3 Tbsp. flour
2 tsp. vanilla

Mix together first three ingredients and press firmly into 9" x 13" pan which has been sprayed with non-stick coating. Bake 5 minutes at 325 degrees. Combine coconut, nuts, 2/3 cup fruit sweetener and lemon juice. In separate bowl, beat eggs with wire whip. Add flour and blend. Beat in vanilla. Add this mixture to the nut mixture and pour over baked crust.Bake 20-25 minutes at 325 degrees. If desired, drizzle over cooked bars 3 Tbsp. lemon juice and 3 Tbsp. fruit sweetener.

Makes 36 bars.

1 bar = 1/2 bread, 1 fat exchanges
80 calories   4 grams fat
9 grams carb.   38 mg sodium
2 grams protein   15 mg cholesterol

LAYERED BARS

A colorful Christmas cookie!

> 1/4 cup margarine
> 1 cup graham cracker crumbs or corn flake crumbs
> 1/2 cup evaporated milk(skimmed)
> 1/2 cup fruit sweetener
> 2 tsp. vanilla
> 2/3 cup chopped nuts
> 2/3 cup shredded coconut
> 1 cup chocolate chips sweetened with barley malt
> 1 cup chopped mixed dried fruit (optional)

Combine margarine and cracker crumbs. Press into bottom of 9" x 9" pan. In sauce pan combine evaporated milk and fruit sweetener. Stir over medium heat until thick (approx. 15 minutes). Add vanilla. Pour over cracker crumb crust. Top with nuts, coconut, chocolate chips, and fruit. Bake 15-20 minutes at 350 degrees.

Makes 16 squares.

1 square = 1 bread, 2 fat exchanges
178 calories	10 grams fat
21 grams carb.	90 mg sodium
3 grams protein	0 mg cholesterol

Note: If dried fruit is included, add 22 calories and 6 grams carb. per square. Increase to 1 bread, 1/2 fruit, 2 fat exchanges

PUMPKIN BARS

A different treat during those autumn holidays!

> 1/2 cup margarine
> 1/2 cup fruit sweetener
> 1/2 cup mashed banana (1 medium banana)
> 1 egg
> 1/2 cup canned pumpkin
> 2 tsp. vanilla
> 1 1/2 cup flour
> 1 tsp. cinnamon
> 1 tsp. each ginger, allspice, baking soda
> 1/2 cup raisins
> 1/2 cup chopped nuts

TOPPING:
> 3 Tbsp. orange juice concentrate
> 3 Tbsp. fruit sweetener
> 2 tsp. orange rind
> 1 tsp. vanilla

Combine margarine, fruit sweetener, and mashed banana. Beat in egg, pumpkin and vanilla. Combine dry ingredients and stir into pumpkin mixture. Add raisins and nuts. Spread into 9" x 13" pan which has been sprayed with a non-stick coating. Bake 20-25 minutes at 325 degrees or until firm in center. Combine juice concentrate, 3 Tbsp. fruit sweetener, orange rind and 1 tsp. vanilla. Spread glaze over warm bars.

Makes 36 bars.

1 bar = 2/3 bread, 1 fat exchanges
78 calories   4 grams fat
10 grams carb.   54 mg sodium
1 gram protein   8 mg cholesterol

LEMON TEA CAKES

A nice cookie with afternoon tea!

1 1/4 cup flour
1/2 tsp. salt
1/4 tsp. baking powder
3 egg whites
1/3 cup fruit sweetener
1/2 cup margarine
3 egg yolks
1/3 cup lemon juice
2 Tbsp. grated lemon rind
1/2 cup nuts (chopped)
1/4 cup Fruit Sweet

Mix together flour, salt, and baking powder. Set aside. Beat egg whites until they mound and set aside. In separate bowl, cream margarine and 1/3 cup fruit sweetener. Beat in egg yolks and lemon juice. Fold in flour mixture. Gently, fold in egg whites, lemon rind, and 1/2 cup nuts. Spread with rubber spatula in 9" x 13" pan which has been lightly greased. Bake 15-18 minutes at 350 degrees. Remove from oven when center springs back if touched. When slightly cool, drizzle with 1/4 cup fruit sweetener. Sprinkle with chopped nuts.(optional).

Makes 36 cakes.

1 cake = 1/3 bread, 1 fat exchanges
66 calories   4 grams fat
6 grams carb.   64 mg sodium
2 grams protein   23 mg cholesterol

GRAHAM GOODIES

Thank you Karen, for this delicious recipe. The first time I made these I couldn't stop nibbling on them.

Filling:

> 2/3 cup evaporated milk (skimmed)
> 2/3 cup fruit sweetener
> 2 Tbsp. cornstarch
> 1 egg
> 1/2 cup shredded coconut
> 1/2 cup chopped nuts
> 1/2 cup chopped dates
> 1 cup graham cracker crumbs
> 1 tsp. vanilla

Line 9" x 13" pan with whole graham cookies.* Set aside. Combine milk and fruit sweetener in saucepan. Add cornstarch and blend well. Beat in egg. Stirring constantly, over medium heat, cook until mixture becomes thick. Remove from heat and add coconut, nuts, dates, crumbs, and vanilla. Spread over crackers. Top with another layer of crackers. Frost entire dessert with 2/3 cup of CREAM CHEESE FROSTING, if desired.

* 16 squares total top and bottom.

Makes 36 bars.

1 bar = 1/2 bread, 1/2 fat exchanges
56 calories   2 grams fat
8 grams carb.   25 mg sodium
1 gram protein   8 mg cholesterol

ANGEL'S PILLOWS

These are so heavenly you'll dream for more when they're gone!

LAYER ONE:
  1/2 cup margarine
  1/2 cup fruit sweetener
  1 1/4 cup flour
LAYER TWO:
  2/3 cup chopped nuts
  1 cup chopped apples (2 medium)
  1/2 cup raisins
  1/2 cup fruit sweetener
  2 Tbsp. rum flavoring
LAYER THREE:
  3 egg whites
  1 tsp. cream of tartar
  3 Tbsp. fruit sweetener
  2 tsp. vanilla

Combine the first three ingredients. Press into bottom of 9" x 13" oblong cake pan. Blend chopped nuts, chopped apples, raisins, fruit sweetener, and rum flavoring. Pour over crust. Bake 10 minutes at 350 degrees. Beat egg whites and cream of tartar until stiff. While still beating, slowly add fruit sweetener and vanilla. Spread meringue over bars. Bake 5 additional minutes or until golden . Cool and cut into squares.

Makes 30 squares.

1 square = 1 fruit, 1 fat exchanges
100 calories   5 grams fat
14 grams carb.   40 mg sodium
2 grams protein   0 mg cholesterol

DATE NUT SQUARES

Traditional bar with a new twist!

Filling:
    2 cups chopped dates
    3/4 cup water
    1/2 cup fruit sweetener

Crust:
    1/2 cup margarine
    1/2 cup fruit sweetener
    1 1/2 cup flour
    1/2 tsp. baking soda
    1 tsp. salt
    1 1/4 cup rolled oats
    1/2 cup chopped nuts

Prepare filling:
In sauce pan, combine 2 cups chopped dates,
3/4 cup water. Cook until thickened. Add 1/2 cup
fruit sweetener and cook 5 minutes more. Let cool.

Crust:
Cream together margarine and second 1/2 cup
fruit sweetener. In separate bowl blend flour,
baking soda, and salt. Add to creamed mixture.
Add rolled oats and nuts. Press half of mixture
in bottom of 9" x 13" pan, which has been sprayed
with non-stick coating. Spread with filling. Top
with remaining crumb mixture. Bake 20 minutes at
350 degrees.

Makes 24 squares.

1 square = 1 bread, 1/2 fruit, 1 fat exchanges
160 calories   6 grams fat
26 grams carb.   143 mg sodium
3 grams protein   0 mg cholesterol

APRICOT BARS

Following BASIC DATE-NUT SQUARES recipe, use the following filling:

    1 1/4 cup chopped apricots
    3/4 cup water
    1/4 cup fruit sweetener
    1/2 cup chopped nuts

Combine ingredients in sauce pan. Cook until thickened. Add nuts. Cool.Spread on crust and add remaining crumb topping. Bake 25 minutes at 350 degrees.

Makes 24 squares.

1 square = 1 bread, 1 fat exchanges
145 calories   7 grams fat
18 grams carb.   143 mg sodium
3 grams protein   0 mg cholesterol

FRUIT CHEWS

A hearty snack! Great for joggers and skiers.

>   1 egg + 3 egg whites
>   2/3 cup fruit sweetener
>   1/2 cup mashed banana (1 medium)
>   1 cup shredded coconut
>   1/2 cup chopped nuts
>   1 cup chopped dates
>   1/2 cup golden raisins
>   1 cup flour
>   1/2 cup wheat germ

Mix eggs, fruit sweetener, and banana. Add
coconut, nuts, dates, and raisins. Stir in flour
and wheat germ. Spread in 9" x 13" pan which has
been sprayed with non-stick coating spray. Bake
at 325 degrees for 20-25 minutes, or until firmly
set in center. Cool before cutting into squares.

Makes 36 bars.

1 bar = 1 bread exchanges
80 calories   2 grams fat
14 grams carb.   13 mg sodium
2 grams protein   7 mg cholesterol

NOTES

CAKES ∼ FROSTINGS

BELVA'S BAVARIAN CAKE

An adaptation of Belva's great chocolate cake. This old country recipe gives it a moist texture and a rich flavor.

>   2/3 cup fruit sweetener
>   1/3 cup unsweetened apple sauce
>   3/4 cup water
>   1/2 cup low-fat ricotta cheese
>   1/4 cup mayonnaise
>   1/4 cup non-fat yogurt (plain)
>   1/4 cup fruit sweetened fudge sauce
>   3 Tbsp. cocoa
>   1 3/4 cup flour
>   2 tsp. baking baking soda
>   2 tsp. vanilla

Cream fruit sweetener, apple sauce, water, ricotta, mayonnaise, and yogurt. Blend well. Stir in fudge sauce and cocoa. Combine flour and baking soda separately, and add to batter. Blend in vanilla. Pour into 9" spring form pan which has been sprayed with non-stick coating. Bake 30-40 minutes at 350 degrees.

Serves 16.

1 serving = 1 1/2 bread, 1/2 fat exchanges
132 calories   3 grams fat
22 grams carb.   135 mg sodium
3 grams protein   5 mg cholesterol

BANANA CAKE

Bananas make this a very sweet heavy cake.

    1/2 cup margarine
    2/3 cup fruit sweetener
    2 eggs
    2 ripe bananas, mashed
    2 tsp. vanilla
    1/4 cup sour cream or ricotta cheese
    1 1/2 cup flour
    1/2 tsp. baking soda
    1 tsp. baking powder
    1/2 tsp. salt
    1/2 cup chopped nuts
    1/2 cup shredded coconut (optional)

Cream margarine and fruit sweetener. Beat in eggs, one at a time. Blend in bananas, vanilla, and sour cream. Separately, combine dry ingredients and add to creamed mixture. Add nuts. Pour into 9" x 9" pan which has been sprayed with non-stick coating. Bake 20-25 minutes at 350 degrees (or until cake springs back when lightly touched).

Serves 16.

1 serving = 1 bread, 2 fat exchanges
188 calories   11 grams fat
20 grams carb.   193 mg sodium
3 grams protein   36 mg cholesterol

Note: Addition of coconut adds 15 calories, 1 gram carb., 1 gram fat per serving.

CARROT CAKE

Another wonderful recipe from my Mom. She is always faithful to send recipes that are especially tasty and good for you!

3/4 cup vegetable oil
3/4 cup fruit sweetener
1 egg + 3 egg whites
2 tsp. vanilla
1 cup crushed pineapple (in its' own juice) including juice
2 cups flour
2 tsp. baking soda
1 tsp. salt
2 tsp. cinnamon
1 cup shredded coconut
2 cups raw shredded carrots
2/3 cup chopped nuts

Blend oil, fruit sweetener, eggs, and vanilla. Beat well. Stir in pineapple. Combine flour, baking soda, salt, and cinnamon. Add to blended mixture. Stir in coconut, carrots, and nuts. Pour into 9" x 13" cake pan which has been sprayed with non-stick coating. Bake at 350 degrees for 30-40 minutes. Cool and frost with CREAM CHEESE FROSTING.

Serves 24.

1 serving = 1 bread, 2 fat exchanges
174 calories   10 grams fat
17 grams carb.   172 mg sodium
3 grams protein   11 mg cholesterol

Note: Frosting adds 30 calories, 5 grams carb., 1 gram protein, 1 gram fat per serving

POPPY SEED ORANGE POUND CAKE

An easy to fix standby for those unexpected occasions!

    3/4 cup margarine
    1/2 cup fruit sweetener
    1/2 cup frozen orange juice concentrate
    1/4 cup unsweetened apple sauce
    3/4 cup plain, non-fat yogurt
    1 tsp. vanilla
    3 egg whites
    2 cups flour
    1 1/2 tsp. baking powder
    1 tsp. salt
    1/4 cup poppy seeds

Combine margarine, fruit sweetener, orange juice concentrate and apple sauce. Beat at low speed with electric mixer until well blended. Add yogurt and vanilla. Beat in egg whites. Combine flour, baking powder, and salt; add to creamed ingredients continuing to beat. Fold in poppyseeds. Pour into 9" x 5" x 3" loaf pan or bundt pan which had been sprayed with non-stick coating. Bake 40-45 minutes at 350 degrees or until cake springs back when lightly touched.

Serves 16.

1 serving = 1 1/2 bread, 2 fat exchanges
186 calories   10 grams fat
21 grams carb.   272 mg sodium
4 grams protein   0 mg cholesterol

ORANGE CHOCOLATE BUNDT CREAM CAKE

Very moist and tasty. Feeds a large group.

    2/3 cup margarine (melted)
    1/2 cup fruit sweetener
    2/3 cup orange juice concentrate
    2/3 cup non-fat yogurt (plain)
    1 egg + 3 egg whites
    2 Tbsp. orange flavoring or orange liquer
    2 cup flour
    1 tsp. salt
    1 tsp. baking powder
    1/2 tsp. baking soda
    1/3 cup fruit sweetened fudge sauce

In large mixing bowl combine first four
ingredients. Blend well with electric mixer. Beat
in eggs, one at a time. Add flavoring. Combine
flour, salt, baking powder, and baking soda. Stir
into creamed mixture. Pour batter into Teflon
coated bundt pan which has been sprayed with
non-stick coating; reserving one cup batter. To
remaining batter, add fudge sauce and blend. Drop
spoonfuls of chocolate batter into orange batter
and marble through with knife. Bake 40-45 minute
at 350 degrees or until cake springs back when
lightly touched. Cool, then invert onto large
plate. Drizzle with 3-4 Tbsp. fudge sauce which
has been heated slightly.

Serves 16.

1 serving = 1 bread, 1 fruit, 1 1/2 fat exchanges
200 calories   8 grams fat
27 grams carb.   277 mg sodium
4 grams protein   17 mg cholesterol

MISSISSIPPI MUD CAKE

A satisfying sweet treat for chocolate lovers.

        2/3 cup margarine
        1/2 cup fruit sweetener
        1/3 cup fruit sweetened fudge sauce
        1/2 cup unsweetened apple sauce
        2 egg whites
        1 1/2 cup flour
        3 Tbsp. cocoa
        2 tsp. vanilla
        1/2 cup shredded coconut
        1/2 cup nuts

Cream margarine, fruit sweetener, fudge sauce, and apple sauce. Beat in egg whites. Combine flour, cocoa and fold in. Stir in vanilla. Add coconut and nuts. Pour into 9" x 9" cakepan which has been sprayed with non-stick coating. Bake 30 to 40 minutes at 350 degrees. While warm spread with 1/3 cup fruit sweetened fudge sauce and sprinkle with more nuts.

Serves 16.

1 serving = 1/2 bread, 1 fruit, 2 fat exchanges
213 calories   12 grams fat
23 grams carb.   100 mg sodium
3 grams protein   0 mg cholesterol

ROCKY ROAD CUPCAKES

A special treat for kids (and chocoholics)!

    1/2 cup margarine (melted)
    1/4 cup cocoa
    2/3 cup fruit sweetener
    2 tsp. vanilla
    2 egg whites
    1 1/4 cups flour
    1 tsp. baking powder
    1 tsp. salt
    1 cup milk
FILLING:
    1/2 cup low-fat Neufchatel
    3 Tbsp. Fruit Sweet
    1 egg white
    2/3 cup chocolate chips, sweetened with
    barley malt

Combine margarine, cocoa, and fruit sweetener in large bowl. Add vanilla and egg whites. Separately, combine flour, baking powder, and salt. Add alternately to batter with 1 cup of milk. Pour into 12 muffin cups which have been sprayed with non-stick coating. Blend Neufchatel and sweetener for filling. Stir in egg, blending well. Add chocolate chips. Drop 1 generous Tbsp. filling into center of each cupcake. Bake 8-10 minutes at 350 degrees. Cool slightly before removing from pan. Spread top of each cupcake with small amount of fruit sweetened fudge sauce if desired.

Makes 12 servings.

1 serving = 1 bread, 1 fruit, 2 fat exchanges
240 calories   12 grams fat
29 grams carb.   345 mg sodium
4 grams protein   8 mg cholesterol

APPLE VALLEY CAKE

Very good warm; topped with whipped cream or ice cream.

- 1/2 cup vegetable oil
- 1/2 cup fruit sweetener
- 1/2 cup unsweetened apple sauce
- 2 eggs
- 1 3/4 cup flour
- 1 tsp. salt
- 2 tsp. baking soda
- 2 tsp. cinnamon
- 4 cups diced apples
- 2/3 cup chopped nuts

Blend together oil, fruit sweetener, and apple sauce. Beat in eggs. Combine dry ingredients separately and stir in. Fold in diced apples and chopped nuts. Pour into 9" x 13" pan which has been sprayed with non-stick coating. Bake 20-30 minutes at 350 degrees. If desired, frost with CREAM CHEESE FROSTING.

Serves 24.

1 serving = 1/3 bread, 1 fruit, 1 fat exchanges
150 calories   7 grams fat
20 grams carb.   156 mg sodium
2 grams protein   23 mg cholesterol

Note: Frosting adds 30 calories, 5 grams carb., 1 gram protein, and 1 gram fat per serving.

DUTCH APPLE CAKE

An "old country" puddin cake. Good topped with whipped cream or ice cream for a warm, yet refreshing, dessert!

> 1/4 cup fruit sweetener
> 1/4 cup Apple Butter or unsweetened apple sauce
> 1 egg
> 2/3 cup flour
> 1/2 tsp. baking powder
> 1/4 tsp. salt
> 1 cup diced apples
> 1/2 cup chopped nuts

Cream fruit sweetener and Apple Butter. Beat in egg. Combine flour, baking powder, and salt. Blend into creamed mixture. Fold in apples and nuts. Pour into 8" x 8" pan which has been sprayed with non-stick coating. Bake for 15-20 minutes at 325 degrees.

Serves 12.

1 serving = 1 fruit, 1 fat exchanges
130 calories   7 grams fat
15 grams carb.   60 mg sodium
4 grams protein   23 mg cholesterol

ROMANTIC DESSERT CAKE

Very different combination, yet very yummy! You
can get hooked on this!

        1 cup chopped dates
        1 cup boiling water
        1 tsp. baking soda
        1/2 cup fruit sweetener
        1/3 cup fruit sweetened fudge sauce
        3/4 cup margarine
        2 eggs
        1 3/4 cup flour
        2 tsp. vanilla
        1/2 cup chopped nuts
        1/2 cup fruit sweetened fudge sauce (24 tsp.)
        or 1/2 cup chocolate chips sweetened with
        barley malt

Combine dates, boiling water, and baking soda in
medium bowl. Let set until cool (about 20
minutes). In separate bowl, cream fruit
sweetener, fudge sauce, and margarine. Beat eggs
in, one at a time. Add flour alternately with
date mixture. Blend in 2 tsp. vanilla. Add
chopped nuts. Pour into 9" x 13" cake pan which
has been sprayed with non-stick coating. Dot with
fudge sauce. Bake 30 to 35 minutes at 325
degrees or until cake springs back when lightly
touched.

Serves 24.

1 serving = 1/2 bread, 1 fruit, 1 1/2 fat exchanges
166 calories   8 grams fat
21 grams carb.   106 mg sodium
2 grams protein   23 mg cholesterol

JUST PEACHY CAKE

I have used this recipe many times for large
school or church groups and it is always well
received.

    1/2 cup margarine
    1/2 cup fruit sweetener
    1/2 cup unsweetened apple sauce
    1 egg
    3/4 cup non-fat yogurt
    1 1/2 cup flour
    1/2 tsp. baking soda
    1/2 tsp. baking powder
    1 1/2 cup sliced peaches
    1 Tbsp. vanilla
TOPPING:
    2 Tbsp. cinnamon
    2 Tbsp. flour
    3 Tbsp. fruit sweetener
    3 Tbsp. mashed potato flakes
    3 Tbsp. melted margarine

Cream together margarine, fruit sweetener,
and apple sauce. Beat in eggs, and yogurt.
Combine dry ingredients separately and fold into
batter. Fold in peaches. Add vanilla. Pour batter
into 9" x 13" cake pan which has been sprayed
with non-stick coating. Sprinkle topping evenly
over cake and bake 25 minutes at 350 degrees.

Serves 24.

1 serving = 1 fruit, 1 fat exchanges
116 calories   6 grams fat
15 grams carb.   94 mg sodium
2 grams protein   12 mg cholesterol

GINGER BRUNCH CAKE

A great dessert, good anytime. Delicious warm,
topped with ice cream or Orange Cream Topping.

        1/2 cup margarine, melted
        1/2 cup fruit sweetener
        1/2 cup unsweetened apple sauce
        1 egg
        3/4 cup plain non-fat yogurt
        1 3/4 cup flour
        1 tsp. baking powder
        1/4 tsp. salt
        2 tsp. cinnamon
        3 tsp. ginger
TOPPING:
        1/4 cup margarine, melted
        1/2 cup instant mashed potato flakes
        1 Tbsp. flour
        3 tsp. cinnamon

Combine margarine, fruit sweetener and apple sauce.
Blend thoroughly. Add egg, and yogurt, beating well.
Combine dry ingredients separately and add to
creamed mixture. Pour into 9" x 9" pan which has
been sprayed with non-stick coating. Combine
topping ingredients; stir with fork until crumbly.
Sprinkle topping on cake batter. Bake 25-30
minutes at 325 degrees.

Serves 16.

1 serving = 1 bread, 2 fat exchanges
176 calories   9 grams fat
21 grams carb.   165 mg sodium
3 grams protein   17 mg cholesterol

CALICO CRUMB CAKE

From my friend, Lorinda, who always makes great
tummy-warming desserts.

> 1/2 cup margarine
> 1/2 cup fruit sweetener
> 2 egg whites
> 1 cup buttermilk
> 2 tsp. vanilla
> 2 cup flour
> 1 tsp. baking soda
> 1 tsp. salt
> 1/2 cup fruit sweetened fudge sauce

TOPPING:
> 1/2 cup flour
> 2 Tbsp. margarine
> 3 Tbsp. fruit sweetener
> 1/2 cup chopped nuts

Cream together margarine and fruit sweetener. Add
two slightly beaten egg whites. Stir in buttermilk
and vanilla. Combine flour, soda, and salt, and add
to batter. Pour batter (reserving 1 cup) into 9" x 13"
cake pan which has been sprayed with non-stick coating.
Blend fudge sauce into remaining cup of batter. Drop
chocolate mixture by spoonfuls over batter. Marble
through with knife. Combine last four ingredients until
crumbly consistency is reached. Sprinkle over top of
cake batter. Bake 30 minutes at 350 degrees, or until
center springs back when slightly touched.

Cut into 20 servings.

1 serving = 1 bread, 1/2 fruit, 1 1/2 fat exchanges
174 calories   8 grams fat
22 grams carb.   223 mg sodium
3 grams protein   trace of cholesterol

OATMEAL CRUNCH CAKE

Heavy and moist. What a treat on a rainy Spring afternoon!

- 1 1/4 cup boiling water
- 1 cup rolled oats
- 1/2 cup margarine
- 1/2 cup fruit sweetener
- 1 tsp. vanilla
- 2 eggs
- 1/2 cup flour
- 1 tsp. baking soda
- 1/2 tsp. salt
- 1 tsp. cinnamon
- 1/2 tsp. nutmeg

CRUNCH TOPPING:
- 1/4 cup margarine (melted)
- 1/3 cup fruit sweetener
- 4 Tbsp. evaporated milk (skimmed)
- 1/3 cup mashed potato flakes or buds
- 1/3 cup chopped nuts
- 1/3 cup shredded coconut

Pour water over rolled oats. Let stand 20 minutes. In separate bowl, combine margarine, fruit sweetener, vanilla. Beat in eggs. Combine dry ingredients separately and add to creamed mixture alternately with oatmeal. Pour into 9" square pan which has been sprayed with non-stick coating. Bake 20 minutes at 350 degrees. Combine topping ingredients, stirring until crumbly. Sprinkle on top of cake and bake an additional 10-15 minutes

Serves 16.

1 serving = 1 bread, 2 fat exchanges
185 calories	12 grams fat
17 grams carb.	230 mg sodium
3 grams protein	34 mg cholesterol

GOLDEN SPICE CAKE

    2 cups flour
    1 tsp. baking powder
    1/2 tsp. soda
    1/2 tsp. salt
    1 tsp. cloves
    1 tsp. nutmeg
    2 tsp. cinnamon
    2/3 cup fruit sweetener
    1/2 cup oil
    1 cup non-fat yogurt
    3 egg whites

Heat oven to 350 degrees. Spray 9" x 13" pan
with non-stick coating spray. Combine first
seven ingredients in large bowl, blending well.
In separate bowl, combine fruit sweetener, oil,
yogurt, Beat two minutes, Add egg whites, one
at a time, beating after each addition. Slowly,
pour this mixture into dry mixture, stirring
until well blended. Pour into baking pan. Bake
20-25 minutes. If desired, top individual servings
with dollop (1 tablespoon) of Fruit Mincemeat,
then a dollop of Fluffy Frosting: 2 egg whites,
beaten until fluffy. Slowly add 2 Tbsp. fruit
sweetener, and 1 Tablespoon real vanilla. Great
substitute for whipped cream!!

Cut cake into 24 servings

1 serving = 1 bread, 1 fat exchanges
103 calories   5 grams fat
13 grams carb.   85 mg sodium
2 grams protein   trace of cholesterol

Note: Addition of 1 tablespoon fruit sweetened
mincemeat adds 30 calories, 5 grams carb. and
1 gram protein per serving.

ANGEL LAYER TORTE

2 cups flour
2 1/2 tsp. baking powder
1/2 tsp salt
1/2 cup vegetable oil
2/3 cup fruit sweetener
1 cup skim milk
2 tsp almond flavoring
4 egg whites

Heat oven to 350 degrees. Spray two round layer
pans with non-stick coating spray. In large bowl
combine oil, fruit sweetener, milk, and flavoring.
Beat well, then add slowly to flour mixture.
Add egg whites, one at a time, beating after each
addition. Beat two minutes. Pour batter into layer
pans. Bake 12-15 minutes. Cool cake slightly
before removing from pans. Stack layers on top
of one another or use fruit juice sweetened preserves *
as filling between layers. If desired, top each
serving with fruit sweetened fudge topping, which has
been heated in microwave.

Makes 20 servings

1 slice = 1 bread, 1 fat exchanges
122 calories   6 grams fat
15 grams carb.   108 mg sodium
2 grams protein   trace of cholesterol

BUTTER ICING

Smooth and creamy!

> 1/3 cup flour
> 1 cup skim milk
> 1/3 cup margarine (softened)
> 2 Tbsp. butter flavoring
> 1/2 cup fruit sweetener
> 2 tsp. vanilla

In small saucepan, blend 1/3 cup flour and 1/3
cup milk. When consistency becomes smooth paste,
add remainder of milk, 2 Tbsp. at a time; beating
well after each addition. Cook over medium heat,
stirring constantly. When mixture becomes thick
paste, remove from heat. Cover and place in
refrigerator. When mixture is cool, scoop into
large bowl. Then add margarine and butter flavoring.
Beat with electric beater. Slowly, add fruit sweetener
and vanilla while continually beating until smooth.
Spread over cooled cake.

Makes approximately 2 1/4 cups frosting.

Entire recipe = 8 fruit, 12 fat exchanges
1/4 cup = 1 fruit, 1 fat exchanges
120 calories   7 grams fat
13 grams carb.   92 mg sodium
2 grams protein   0 mg cholesterol

PEANUT BUTTER ICING
Delicious on any simple cake. Especially great
on graham crackers!

To make Butter Icing and add 3 Tbsp. peanut butter
in place of 2 Tbsp. margarine
Makes approximately 2 1/4 cups frosting.

Note: Nutrient values are not significantly
changed from butter icing.

CHOCOLATE ICING

Great on Chocolate Brownies!

    1/3 cup flour
    1 cup milk
    1/3 cup margarine, softened
    1/2 cup fruit sweetened fudge sauce
    2 Tbsp. fruit sweetener
    2 tsp. vanilla
    1 tsp. orange flavoring or Grand Marnier if
    desired

In small saucepan, blend 1/3 cup flour and 1/2 cup milk. When consistency becomes smooth paste, add remaining milk, 2 Tbsp. at a time, beating well after each addition. Cook over medium heat, stirring constantly, until mixture becomes thick paste. Remove from heat and cool covered in refrigerator. When mixture has cooled, scoop into large bowl (use rubber scraper). Add margarine, fudge sauce, and fruit sweetener and beat with electric mixer until smooth. Beat in flavorings. Spread on cooled cake.

Makes approximately 2 cups frosting.

Total recipe = 10 fruit, 12 fat exchanges
1/4 cup = 1 fruit, 2 fat exchanges
154 calories   8 grams fat
18 grams carb.   103 mg sodium
2 grams protein   trace of cholesterol

CREAM CHEESE FROSTING

A must on Carrot Cake or Bunny's Chocolate Cookies!

>	1/3 cup flour
>	1 cup skim milk
>	2/3 cup fruit sweetener
>	1/3 cup low-fat Neufchatel (3 ozs) (softened)
>	1 Tbsp. margarine
>	2 tsp. vanilla

Combine flour and 1/4 cup of milk in small saucepan. Blend together into smooth paste. Slowly, add remaining milk and beat until smooth. Cook over medium heat, stirring constantly until mixture becomes thick paste. Cover and cool in refrigerator. When cool, scoop mixture into large bowl. Blend fruit sweetener, Neufchatel, and margarine into thickened mixture. Beat with electric mixer. Stir in vanilla. Spread on cake or cookies. For variety, add 1 Tbsp. Amaretto or 1 Tbsp. Grand Marnier.

Makes 2 cups

Entire recipe = 7 bread, 2 fruit, 7 fat exchanges
1/4 cup = 1 bread, 1 fat exchanges

120 calories	4 grams fat
17 grams carb.	75 mg sodium
3 grams protein	9 mg cholesterol

ORANGE CREAM CHEESE FROSTING

Follow above directions. When blending in fruit sweetener, add 2 Tbsp. orange juice concentrate along with other ingredients. Makes 2 cups

Addition of orange juice concentrate adds 5 calories and 1 gram carb. for 1/4 cup frosting

SPICED ICING

Great on Apple Cake!

1/3 cup flour
1 cup skim milk
1/2 cup fruit sweetener
3 Tbsp. margarine (softened)
2 tsp. vanilla
1 tsp. cinnamon
1 tsp. ginger
1 tsp. allspice

Combine flour and 1/4 cup milk in saucepan. Blend into smooth paste. Slowly, add remaining milk and beat well. Stir in fruit sweetener. Cook over medium heat, stirring constantly, until mixture becomes thick paste. Remove from heat, cover, and cool in refrigerator. When cool, scoop mixture into large bowl. Add remaining ingredients and beat with electric mixer until smooth. Spread on cake or cookies. Refrigerate any unused portion.

Makes approximately 2 cups frosting.

Entire recipe = 4 bread, 4 fruit, 7 fat exchanges
1/4 cup = 1 bread, 1 fat exchanges
106 calories   4 grams fat
15 grams carb.   65 mg sodium
2 grams protein   0 mg cholesterol

COCONUT-NUT FROSTING

Great for turning an ordinary chocolate cake into a German Chocolate cake!

2/3 cup evaporated skim milk
2/3 cup fruit sweetener
2 egg yolks (slightly beaten)
3 Tbsp. margarine
2 tsp. vanilla
3/4 cup shredded coconut
3/4 cup chopped almonds (30 whole almonds)

Combine skim milk, fruit sweetener, egg yolks, and margarine in saucepan until well blended. Cook over medium heat, stirring constantly, until mixture thickens (approximately 10-12 minutes). Remove from heat. Beat in vanilla. Stir in coconut and nuts. Beat until cool.

Makes approximately 3 1/4 cups frosting.

Total recipe = 2 skim milk, 8 bread, 2 fruit, and 24 fat exchanges

1/4 cup frosting = 1 bread, 2 fat exchanges
145 calories   9 grams fat
13 grams carb.   61 mg sodium
3 grams protein   42 mg cholesterol

Pies ⌃ Pastries

CRUMB CRUST

1 Tbsp Canola Oil
7 tsp. fruit sweetener
2 Tbsp finely chopped almonds
1 1/4 cup potato flakes
2-3 Tbsp. water

Combine oil, fruit sweetener, and almonds. Add potato flakes and mix with fork until well blended. Add enough water to make mixture slightly moist. Press into 8" or 9" pie tin. If using for an unbaked pie (such as Lemon Meringue) bake 5-8 minutes at 350 degrees. If using for Cheesecake or baked fruit pie, fill, and then bake as directed. Great and tasty calorie cutter, for any pie recipe. If desired, this mixture can also be used as a crumb topping for any fruit pie. Just mix, and sprinkle by hand over fruit.

For whole recipe:
560 calories   23 grams fat
83 grams carb.   64 mg sodium
8 grams protein   0 mg cholesterol

1 serving (1/8 of recipe) = 1/2 bread, 1/2 fat exchanges
70 calories   3 grams fat
10 grams carb.   8 mg sodium
1 grams protein   0 mg cholesterol

PIE PASTRY

Two crust pie pastry. Thank you Susan Ebel, who taught me the secret to flaky pie crust!

    1 1/2 cup flour
    1/2 tsp. salt
    1/3 cup vegetable shortening or margarine
    2-3 Tbsp. cold water
    2 Tbsp. shortening

Combine flour and salt in large bowl. Cut in 1/4 cup shortening with fork or pastry blender. Add water, a little at a time until dough is moistened. Divide dough in half. Place one portion on pastry cloth, using cloth stocking on rolling pin. Roll into thick 6 inch circle. Spread circle with 1 Tbsp. shortening. Fold in half, then in quarters. Now, roll pastry into large circle to fit pie tin. (the extra shortening adds flakiness to the pastry) Thinner pastry tends to be less tough. Roll out second portion in same manner. Follow desired pie recipe.

Serves 8

1 serving double crust = 1 bread, 2 1/2 fat exchanges
188 calories   12 grams fat
17 grams carb.   122 mg sodium
3 grams protein   0 mg cholesterol

1 serving single crust = 1/2 bread, 1 fat exchanges
94 calories   6 grams fat
9 grams carb.   60 mg sodium
1 grams protein   0 mg cholesterol

APPLE PIE

Use apples of your choice. I use Granny Smith apples; tart and crisp.

    pastry for 2 crust 9" pie
    6-7 large apples, peeled, cored and sliced
    1/2 cup fruit sweetener
    2 tsp. cinnamon
    1 tsp. nutmeg
    1 Tbsp. margarine

Line pie pan with bottom pastry. In large bowl, combine ingredients except margarine. Mix well and spoon into pastry lined pan. Dot with margarine. Cover with top crust, seal, and flute edges. Cut a few small slits in crust. Bake 40 minutes at 350 degrees, or until crust is golden brown.

Serves 8.

1 serving = 2 bread, 1 fruit, 2 fat exchanges
298 calories   14 grams fat
42 grams carb.   140 mg sodium
3 grams protein   0 mg cholesterol

CHEESE APPLE PIE

Follow directions for Apple Pie. Just before adding top crust, sprinkle 6 Tbsp. fresh grated parmesan cheese over apple mixture. Add top crust etc.

Serves 8.

1 serving = 2 bread, 1 fruit, 3 fat exchanges
320 calories   15 grams fat
43 grams carb.   226 mg sodium
5 grams protein   4 mg cholesterol

CRUMB TOPPED CHERRY PIE

Another Christmas favorite in our family! Crumb topping adds a festive touch. Thank you mom, for another great recipe!

pastry for one-crust pie.
2 (1 lb.) cans red tart cherries
(packed in water)
1/2 cup fruit sweetener
3 Tbsp. cornstarch
1/4 cup water
1/4 tsp. salt
1 tsp. grated lemon peel
2 Tbsp. lemon juice
few drops red food coloring (optional)
2 Tbsp. almond flavoring

TOPPING:
1/4 cup flour
1/2 cup instant mashed potato flakes or buds
1/4 cup fruit sweetener
1 tsp. cinnamon
1/4 tsp. nutmeg
1/4 cup margarine

Line 9" pie pan with prepared pastry. Set aside. Drain cherries, reserving 1 cup liquid. In saucepan, combine cornstarch and 1/4 cup of water, stirring until smooth. Add cherry liquid, fruit sweetener, and salt. Simmer mixture over medium heat, stirring constantly, until it thickens. Remove from heat and add cherries, peel, lemon juice, food coloring and almond flavoring. Pour into prepared pie shell. Combine last six ingredients and blend to crumbly consistency. Sprinkle over pie filling. Bake 30 minutes at 350 degrees. Cut into 12 pieces.

1 serving = 1 bread, 2/3 fruit, 1 1/2 fat
178 calories   8 grams fat
26 grams carb.   128 mg sodium
2 grams protein   0 mg cholesterol

BLUEBERRY PIE

Blueberries have a natural sweetness and are low in sugar!

          pastry for a 2 crust pie
          4 cups fresh blueberries
          1/3 cup fruit sweetener
          1/4 cup flour
          1/2 tsp. nutmeg
          1/2 tsp. cinnamon

Line pie pan with bottom pastry. In large bowl, combine remaining ingredients in order. Pour berry mixture into pastry lined pan. Add top crust. Seal and flute edges. Bake 30-40 minutes at 350 degrees. Cool slightly before serving.

Serves 8.

1 serving = 2 bread, 1/2 fruit, 2 fat exchanges
270 calories   12 grams fat
37 grams carb.   127 mg sodium
3 grams protein   0 mg cholesterol

PEACHES AND CREAM PIE

Adapted from Becky Grey's wonderful recipe! Great
with fresh Washington Peaches!

        1/2 cup fruit sweetener
        1/4 cup quick cooking tapioca
        1/4 tsp. salt
        1/4 tsp. nutmeg
        1 cup skimmed evaporated milk
        pastry for 9" pie (2 crusts)
        4 cups peeled and sliced peaches

In medium bowl, combine fruit sweetener, tapioca,
salt, and nutmeg. Pour evaporated milk over
ingredients, stir well, then let set for 30
minutes. Prepare pie pastry. Place bottom crust
in 9" pie pan. Fill crust with sliced peaches.
Pour milk mixture over peaches. Add top crust and
flute edges. Bake 30-40 minutes (or until crust
is golden) at 375 degrees. Cool completely. Best
when not chilled.

Serves 8.

1 serving = 2 bread, 1 fruit, 2 fat exchanges
306 calories   12 grams fat
44 grams carb.   221 mg sodium
6 grams protein   trace of cholesterol

Note: Can be made as deep dish pie, using only one
crust. Then 1 serving = 1 1/2 bread, 1 fruit, and
1 fat exchanges.

PUMPKIN PIE

Great for a cool crisp autumn evening.

> pastry for one-crust pie
> 1 3/4 cups canned pumpkin
> 1/2 tsp. salt
> 1 1/2 cups evaporated skim milk
> 3 eggs
> 2/3 cup fruit sweetener
> 2 tsp. ginger
> 2 tsp. cinnamon
> 1/2 tsp. nutmeg
> 1/4 tsp. cloves

Heat oven to 350 degrees. Prepare pastry and line 9" pie pan with crust. Flute edge of crust. Combine all ingredients in order and beat two minutes on low with electric mixer. Pour mixture into crust and bake 30-40 minutes or until pie seems set. Cool slightly before serving.

Serves 8.

1 serving = 1 fruit, 1 bread, 1 1/2 fat

230 calories	8 grams fat
31 grams carb.	267 mg sodium
8 grams protein	104 mg cholesterol

MINCE PIE

Very rich. Great warm or cold!

      pastry for 2 crust pie
      1 jar Fruit Mincemeat (Wax Orchards)*
      2 cups apples (chopped)
      1/2 cup raisins
      16 pecan halves, chopped
      3 Tbsp. rum flavoring

Prepare pastry crusts. Line bottom of 8" pie pan.
In large bowl, combine Fruit Mincemeat, apples,
raisins, and pecans. Stir in flavoring until well
mixed. Pour into crust. Roll out top crust, set
over filling and flute crust edge. Bake 30
minutes (until golden) at 350 degrees.

Serves 12.

1 serving = 1 bread, 1 fruit, 2 fat exchanges
228 calories   10 grams fat
32 grams carb.   83 mg sodium
3 grams protein   0 mg cholesterol

* See page 102 for recipe for fruit mincemeat.

MOM'S SOUTHERN PECAN PIE

A great Thanksgiving tradition in our home.

        1 unbaked pie shell
        1 cup fruit sweetener
        1 envelope plain gelatin
        1/3 cup unsweetened apple sauce
        3 Tbsp. water
        2 Tbsp. cornstarch
        3 eggs
        2 tsp. vanilla
        2 Tbsp. very strong coffee or espresso.
        (prepared, not grounds)
        24 pecan halves

Prepare pastry and place in 9" pie pan. In large
bowl, combine fruit sweetener, gelatin and apple
sauce . Beat with electric mixer. In small bowl,
blend water and cornstarch until smooth. Add
cornstarch to fruit sweetener mixture and blend.
Beat in eggs, one at a time. Stir in vanilla and
coffee. Pour mixture into pie shell. Decorate top
with pecan halves. Bake 30-40 minutes (until
custard is set) at 375 degrees.
Cool slightly before cutting.

Serves 10.

1 serving = 1 bread, 1 fruit, 2 fat exchanges
211 calories   9 grams fat
28 grams carb.   69 mg sodium
3 grams protein   82 mg cholesterol

LEMON MERINGUE PIE

Elsie's recipe for lemon meringue pie is the best
I've ever tasted! Thank you, Elsie!

    1 baked and cooled single crust pie shell
    2 cups water
    1/3 cup cornstarch
    1/2 cup fruit sweetener (2/3 for those who
    like it sweet)
    2 egg yolks, slightly beaten
    1 Tbsp. margarine
    2/3 cup lemon juice (approx. 3 large lemons)
    2 tsp. grated lemon peel
MERINGUE:
    4 egg whites
    1/2 tsp. cream of tartar
    2 Tbsp. fruit sweetener
    2 tsp. vanilla

Combine 1/2 cup of water and cornstarch in saucepan.
Add remainder of water and fruit sweetener. Stirring
constantly over medium heat, cook until mixture
thickens and boils. Boil 1 minute. Remove from heat;
stir half of mixture into egg yolks; then blend this
back into hot mixture. Stir and cook 2 more minutes.
Remove from heat and stir in margarine, lemon juice,
and lemon peel. Pour in baked pie shell. Beat egg
whites and cream of tartar until fluffy. Slowly,
add fruit sweetener and continue beating until
stiff and glossy. Beat in vanilla. Heap meringue
onto hot pie filling, sealing meringue to edge of
crust. Bake 5-7 minutes at 350 degrees or until
golden. (Great hot! A little messy, but great!)

Serves 10.

1 serving = 1/2 fruit, 1 bread, 1 1/2 fat exchanges
163 calories   7 grams fat
22 grams carb.   84 mg sodium
3 grams protein   54 mg cholesterol

LEMON CHIFFON PIE

If you like lemon, you'll love this pie!

>1 cups graham cracker crumbs (16 squares)
>3 Tbsp margarine
>3 egg whites
>1/2 tsp. cream of tartar
>1/2 cup fruit sweetener
>3 Tbsp. lemon juice
>1 Tbsp. grated lemon peel
>1/4 cup whipping cream (whipped)

Combine graham cracker crumbs and margarine in small bowl. Press mixture into 9" pie pan. Bake 5 minutes at 350 degrees. Cool. In medium bowl beat egg whites and cream of tartar until fluffy. Slowly, add fruit sweetener and lemon juice. Continue beating until stiff. Fold in lemon peel and whipped cream. Spoon mixture into pie crust. Chill or freeze. When ready to serve, top each serving with Berry Sauce (see Berry Sauce recipe).

Makes 10 servings.

1 serving = 1 bread, 1 fat exchanges
132 calories   6 grams fat
16 grams carb.   110 mg sodium
2 grams protein   8 mg cholesterol

BANANA CREAM PIE

An adaptation of Vicki Bilyeu's delicious recipe.
Thank you, Vicki.

    1 baked pastry shell (single)
    1/4 cup cornstarch
    2 cups cold skim milk
    1/4 tsp. salt
    1/2 cup fruit sweetener
    2 egg yolks, beaten
    1 Tbsp. margarine
    2 tsp. vanilla
    3 egg whites
    2 bananas
MERINGUE:
    3 egg whites
    1 tsp. cream of tartar
    2 Tbsp. Fruit Sweet
    2 tsp. vanilla

In top of double boiler, combine cornstarch and
1/2 cup of milk. When blended, add remainder of
milk plus salt and fruit sweetener. Cook in double
boiler until thick, stirring constantly. Slowly,
add small amount of hot mixture to egg yolks. Stir
egg yolk mixture back into hot mixture and cook 2
minutes more. Remove from heat and add margarine
and vanilla. Cool thoroughly. Beat egg whites
until stiff, then fold into pudding mixture. Add
bananas and pour into pastry shell. To make the
meringue topping (optional), beat egg whites and
cream of tartar, until fluffy. Slowly, add fruit
sweetener and vanilla. Beat until stiff. Pour onto
pie and bake 5 minutes at 375 degrees (or until golden).

Makes 12 servings.

1 serving = 1 fruit, 1/2 bread, 1 fat exchanges
164 calories   6 grams fat
23 grams carb.   140 mg sodium
5 grams protein   46 mg cholesterol

BARBARA'S BERRY PIE

Thank you Barbara! Great with strawberries, blueberries, or blackberries.

> 6 egg whites
> 1/2 tsp. cream of tartar
> 8 Tbsp. fruit sweetener
> 2 cups berries (fresh berries work better than frozen)

In large deep bowl, beat three of the egg whites and cream of tartar until fluffy. Slowly, add 3 Tbsp. fruit sweetener and beat until stiff. Spoon meringue into 9" pie pan, spreading meringue evenly to form a crust. Bake this crust 1 hour at 250 degrees. Cool. Mix 2 cups fresh berries (slice berries if using strawberries) with 2 Tbsp. fruit sweetener, or sweeten to taste. Spoon berries onto crust. In deep bowl, beat remaining three egg whites until fluffy. Add remaining 3 Tbsp. fruit sweetener and beat until mixture peaks. Spoon mounds of meringue over berries, spreading to edge of crust. Bake 2-3 minutes at 450 degrees or until meringue is golden. Serve immediately. Light and delicious.

Makes 8 servings.

1 serving = 1 fruit exchange
62 calories   0 grams fat
12 grams carb.   38 mg sodium
3 grams protein   0 mg cholesterol

CHOCOLATE MOOSE PIE

I never met a Chocolate "Moose" I didn't like!

    1 baked 8" or 9" pie shell
    1 Chocolate Pudding recipe (locate in index)
    (cooled)
    3 egg whites
    1 tsp. cream of tartar
    2 tsp. vanilla

Prepare pie shell; cool. Prepare pudding; cool.
Beat egg whites and cream of tartar until very
fluffy. Beat in vanilla, until egg whites hold
stiff peaks. Fold in pudding until just mixed.
Pour into prepared pie shell and chill 1 hour.
Top with finely chopped nuts or toasted slivered
almonds. Caution: tends to break down if stored
too long.

Serves 8.

1 serving = 1 fruit, 1 bread, 1 fat exchanges
192 calories   7 grams fat
27 grams carb.   248 mg sodium
5 grams protein   trace of cholesterol

PEANUT BUTTER PIE

This is so rich! A small piece is very satisfying.

    1 cups graham cracker crumbs (16 squares)
    1 Tbsp. margarine
    1/2 cup fruit sweetener
    1/2 cup peanut butter (chunky)
    2/3 cup low-fat Neufchatel
    4 eggs whites
    1/2 tsp. cream of tartar
    1 Tbsp. fruit sweetener
    1/3 cup mashed potato flakes

Combine graham cracker crumbs and margarine.
Press into 9 inch pie pan. Bake 5 minutes at 350
degrees. Cool. In large bowl, cream fruit
sweetener, peanut butter, and Neufchatel. Beat
until smooth. Set aside. Beat egg whites and
cream of tartar until stiff. Slowly, add fruit
sweetener. Fold in potato flakes. With rubber
spatula, fold entire egg white mixture into
peanut butter batter. When well blended, pour
mixture into cooled pie crust. Refrigerate 1
hour. Very rich!

Makes 12 pieces.

1 piece = 1 bread, 2 fat exchanges
182 calories   10 grams fat
17 grams carb.   174 mg sodium
6 grams protein   10 mg cholesterol

DESSERTS ∧ DECADENCE

NOTES

CHRISTMAS TORTE

Adapted from a German recipe.

1 1/2 cups flour
1 tsp. baking powder
3 Tbsp margarine
1 cup fruit sweetener as specified
1 egg
1 pkg. unflavored gelatin
1 cup mashed raspberries (1 cup after
mashing)
3 Tbsp margarine
2 egg whites
1/2 cup finely ground blanched almonds (40)
1/3 cup flour
1 tsp. almond flavoring

Blend flour and baking powder. Combine margarine
and 1/4 cup fruit sweetener and add this to flour
mixture. Add 1 egg and blend with fork until smooth.
Press dough evenly in 10 inch springform pan or tort
pan which has been sprayed with non-stick coating.
Sprinkle gelatin over raspberries and stir until
dissolved. Combine mashed raspberries and 1/4 cup
fruit sweetener, mixing well. Spread this mixture on
crust. Cream margarine and 1/2 cup fruit sweetener.
Add 2 egg whites, one at a time. Beat well. Mix in
ground almonds, flour, and almond flavoring. Spoon
filling on top of raspberries (crust). Bake 35
minutes at 350 degrees. Cool in pan. If desired,
spoon a few raspberries over individual servings.

Makes 16 servings.

1 serving = 1/2 bread, 1 fruit, 1 1/2 fat exchanges
166 calories   7 grams fat
22 grams carb.   82 mg sodium
3 grams protein   17 mg cholesterol

CHOCOLATE PUDDING

A traditional dessert with a rich chocolate flavor!

    3 Tbsp. cornstarch
    1/2 tsp. salt
    2 cups skim milk
    1/2 cup fruit sweetened fudge topping
    2 tsp. margarine
    1 tsp. vanilla

In medium saucepan, combine cornstarch, salt, and
1/2 cup cold milk. Blend this mixture until smooth
and add remainder of milk and fruit sweetened fudge
topping. Stir constantly over medium heat until mixture
thickens and begins to boil.* Remove from heat and add
margarine and vanilla. Pour into serving dishes.

Makes 4 servings.

1 serving = 1 fruit, 1 skim milk exchanges
178 calories   2 grams fat
31 grams carb.   329 mg sodium
4 grams protein   trace of cholesterol

*For a richer pudding: When you remove from heat
pour small amount of pudding over 2 beaten egg
yolks, which have been placed in small bowl.
Return entire mixture to saucepan, cook 2
minutes, then remove from heat and add 2 Tbsp.
margarine and vanilla.

Note: For richer version, add 60 calories,
138 mg cholesterol, 8 grams fat.

RICH VANILLA PUDDING

For a special treat, add sliced bananas to
finished pudding.

> 3 Tbsp. cornstarch
> 2 cups skim milk
> 1/2 cup fruit sweetener
> 1/4 tsp. salt
> 1 egg yolk (beaten)
> 2 tsp. margarine
> 2 tsp. vanilla

Combine in medium saucepan, cornstarch and 1/2
cup milk. When smoothly blended, add fruit
sweetener, salt, and remaining milk. Stirring
constantly over medium heat, cook until mixture
thickens and begins to bubble. Pour part of
pudding over egg yolk and blend. Blend egg yolk
mixture back into hot mixture in saucepan. Cook 2
additional minutes. Remove from heat. Blend in
margarine and vanilla. Pour into serving dishes.
Serve warm or cool.

Makes 4 servings.

1 serving = 1/2 skim milk, 1 fruit exchange
149 calories   4 grams fat
23 grams carb.   200 mg sodium
5 grams protein   70 mg cholesterol

CHOCOLATE MOUSSE

This is my favorite! Very rich, yet few calories!
You won't believe how good this is!

> 1/2 cup fruit sweetened fudge sauce
> 1 pkg. unflavored gelatin
> 1/4 cup water
> 1/2 square unsweetened chocolate
> 2 Tbsp. fruit sweetener
> 4 egg whites
> 1/4 tsp. cream of tartar
> dash salt
> 2 tsp. vanilla or rum flavoring

Place fudge sauce in medium bowl. Set aside.
Combine gelatin and water in small bowl until
gelatin is dissolved. On double boiler melt 1/2
square chocolate, Add dissolved gelatin and fruit
sweetener. Remove from heat. Beat with rubber
spatula until mixture is slightly cooled. (2
minutes) Pour chocolate mixture into fudge sauce.
Mix thoroughly. In separate bowl, combine egg
whites, cream tartar, and salt, Beat egg whites
until peak forms. Beating at low speed, add
spoonfuls of chocolate mixture until completely
blended. Add flavoring and spoon into 6 dessert
dishes. If desired sprinkle with chopped roasted
almonds.

Makes 6 servings.

1 serving = 1 fruit, 1/2 lean meat exchanges
100 calories   1 gram fat
17 grams carb.   66 mg sodium
3 grams protein   0 mg cholesterol

CHOCOLATE-EE-CLAIRS

Kids love this special treat! It's healthy for them, too!

PUFFS:
>   1/2 cup margarine
>   1 1/8 cups water
>   1 cup flour
>   dash salt
>   4 eggs

FILLING:
>   3 Tbsp. cornstarch
>   2 cups skim milk
>   1/3 cup fruit sweetener
>   1 Tbsp. margarine
>   2 tsp. rum flavoring
>   2 egg whites
>   1/4 tsp cream of tartar

Combine margarine and water in saucepan. Bring to boil. Add flour and salt, constantly stirring over low heat. Remove from heat and add eggs, one at a time. Stir well with each addition. With large spoon, scoop dough onto Teflon baking sheet, making 12 puffs. Bake 25-35 minutes at 400 degrees. Cool. In large saucepan combine cornstarch with 1/2 cup of milk until well blended. Add remaining milk and fruit sweetener. Stirring constantly, bring pudding to boil. Remove from heat and add margarine and flavoring. Cool completely. Beat egg whites and cream of tartar and fold into cooled pudding. Slice top off each puff. Fill with pudding and replace top. Drizzle with warmed fruit sweetened fudge sauce.

Makes 12 ee-clairs.

1 ee-clair = 1 fruit, 1/2 skim milk 2 fat exchanges
181 calories	10 grams fat
16 grams carb.	168 mg sodium
5 grams protein	92 mg cholesterol

DATE TORTE

Another winter holiday favorite. Great with spiced tea!

    1 cup finely chopped dates (approx. 12 dates)
    2/3 cup chopped nuts
    3 Tbsp. cracker crumbs
    4 egg whites
    1 tsp. cream of tartar
    1/2 cup fruit sweetener
    1/2 tsp baking powder
    dash salt
    1 tsp. vanilla

In small bowl, mix dates, nuts, cracker crumbs; set aside. In large mixing bowl, beat egg whites until fluffy. Add cream of tartar. Continue beating egg whites until stiff. In slow stream add fruit sweetener. Beat in baking powder, salt, and vanilla. Fold in date mixture. Pour into 8" x 8" pan which has been sprayed with non-stick coating. Bake 20-30 minutes at 350 degrees. Top with whipped cream.

Makes 12 pieces.

1 piece = 1 fruit, 1 fat exchanges
117 calories   4 grams fat
19 grams carb.   57 mg sodium
3 grams protein   trace of cholesterol

Note: Whipped cream not included in nutrient values.

FRUIT AND CAKE DELIGHT

Great right from the oven on a cool autumn evening. Another of Grandma Audrey's fruit desserts! Great with fresh Italian plums (the dark purple ones).

    2 cups blueberries
    1/4 cup fruit sweetener
    1/2 cup fruit sweetener
    1/2 cup vegetable oil
    2 egg whites
    2 tsp. vanilla
    1 cup flour
    2 tsp. baking powder
    1/4 tsp. salt

Combine fruit and 1/4 cup fruit sweetener. Spoon fruit into 9" x 9" pan and set aside. Combine in medium bowl: 1/2 cup fruit sweetener, oil, and egg whites. Blend well. Add vanilla. Combine dry ingredients separately and add to batter. Pour batter over fruit. Bake 30 minutes at 350 degrees. Topping of whipped cream or French Vanilla Ice Cream is terrific on this warm dessert.

Makes 12 pieces.

1 piece = 1 fruit, 1/2 bread, 2 fat exchanges
175 calories   10 grams fat
21 grams carb.   107 mg sodium
2 grams protein   0 mg cholesterol

GINGERBREAD

Great warm with Orange-Cream Cheese Frosting (see
sauces & toppings & goodies).

     1/2 cup margarine
     2/3 cup fruit sweetener
     1/2 cup non-fat yogurt
     2 egg whites
     2 cups flour
     1 tsp. baking soda
     dash salt
     1 tsp. ginger
     1 tsp. cinnamon
     1 tsp. allspice

In large bowl, cream together margarine, fruit
sweetener, and yogurt. When well blended, beat
in eggs whites. Combine dry ingredients separately
and add to batter. Pour into 9x9 inch pan which
has been sprayed with non-stick coating. Bake 30
minutes at 350 degrees.

Makes 16 pieces.

1 piece = 1 bread, 1 1/2 fat exchanges
140 calories   6 grams fat
19 grams carb.   140 mg sodium
3 grams protein   trace of cholesterol

SOUTHERN SUMMER COBBLER

One of Grandma Audrey's specialities! Works well
with most fruit, but especially good with fresh
blackberries.

> 1/3 cup margarine
> 1 cup flour
> 1 1/2 tsp. baking powder
> 1/2 cup fruit sweetener
> 3/4 cup water
> 2 cups blackberries or other fruit
> 1/4 cup fruit sweetener (adjust to sweetness
> of fruit)
> 2 tsp. almond flavoring

In 9"x 9" pan melt margarine. Set aside. Combine
flour and baking powder in small bowl. Add
fruit sweetener and water. Mix well. Pour batter
over melted margarine. In another bowl, combine
fruit, fruit sweetener, and flavoring. Blend
together, then pour fruit mixture over batter.
Bake 25 minutes at 350 degrees.

Makes 12 servings.

1 serving = 1 fruit, 1/2 bread, 1 fat exchanges
134 calories   5 grams fat
20 grams carb.   100 mg sodium
1 gram protein   0 mg cholesterol

CHEESECAKE

This recipe contains all the taste without all the calories!

    3/4 cups graham cracker crumbs
    2 Tbsp. margarine (melted)

Mix well and press into bottom of 8" springform pan.

    2 cups low-fat ricotta cheese
    2/3 cup low-fat Neufchatel
    1/3 cup fruit sweetener
    1/3 cup mashed potato flakes
    1/3 cup non-fat yogurt
    1 tsp. vanilla
    4 egg whites

With electric mixer, beat ricotta and Neufchatel well. Add fruit sweetener, potato flakes, and yogurt. Continue beating while adding vanilla. Beat 3 minutes. In separate bowl, beat egg whites until they hold peaks. Fold into cheese mixture. Pour into crust and sprinkle with nutmeg. Bake 40 to 50 minutes at 350 degrees until cheesecake is slightly firm in center. Cool before slicing.

Serves 12.

1 serving = 1 skim milk, 1 1/2 fat exchanges
162 calories   9 grams fat
13 grams carb.   175 mg sodium
8 grams protein   23 mg cholesterol

FROSTY CHOCOLATE CHEESECAKE

Rich, moist, and especially chocolate!

CRUST:
> 3/4 cup graham cracker crumbs
> 2 Tbsp. melted margarine

Combine and press into bottom of 8" or 9" spring form pan.

FILLING:
> 1-16 oz. carton low-fat ricotta
> 1/2 cup low-fat Neufchatel
> 1/2 cup fruit sweetened fudge sauce
> 1/3 cup mashed potato flakes
> 2 tsp. vanilla
> 3 egg whites
> 1/2 cup fruit sweetener
> 1/2 cup chopped pecans (optional)

Combine ricotta, Neufchatel, and fudge sauce. Stir in potato flakes and vanilla. In separate bowl, beat egg whites until fluffy. Continue beating and slowly add fruit sweetener. Fold egg whites and, if desired, chopped pecans into cheese batter. Pour into crust and place in freezer for 6 hours. Remove from freezer 20 minutes before serving.

Makes 12 servings.

1 serving = 1 1/2 fruit, 1 lean meat, 1 fat exchanges
190 calories   8 grams fat
21 grams carb.   154 mg sodium
7 grams protein   19 mg cholesterol

Note: Addition of nuts adds 32 calories and 3 grams fat per serving.

PEACHES AND CREAM CHEESECAKE

Adapted from Peggy Swanstrom's delicious recipe!
Thank you.

CRUST LAYER:
    3/4 cup flour
    1 tsp. baking powder
    1/2 tsp. salt
    4 Tbsp. margarine, melted
    3 Tbsp. fruit sweetener
    1/2 cup skim milk
    1 egg
    2 peaches, sliced or 1-16 oz. can of
    sliced sugar-free peaches
SECOND LAYER:
    1/4 cup low-fat Neufchatel
    1 cup low-fat ricotta cheese
    1/3 cup fruit sweetener
    1 egg white

Combine dry ingredients and blend well. In
saucepan, heat margarine, fruit sweetener, and
milk until margarine melts. Add to dry mixture.
Blend in one slightly beaten egg. Pour into
9" x 9" pan which has been sprayed with non-
stick coating. On top of this arrange sliced
peaches.

In separate bowl, beat low-fat Neufchatel and
ricotta cheese until fluffy. Add fruit sweetener
and egg white. Blend well. Spoon over crust layer.
Sprinkle with nutmeg. Bake 20 minutes at 350
degrees. Serve warm.

Makes 16 (2 1/2 ") squares.

1 square = 1/2 bread, 1 fat exchanges
100 calories   5 grams fat
9 grams carb.   162 mg sodium
4 grams protein   25 mg cholesterol

BLUEBERRIES AND CREAM CHEESECAKE

Follow directions for PEACHES AND CREAM CHEESCAKE
(p.96) and substitute 1 1/2 cup blueberries
(fresh or frozen) for peach slices.

Makes 16 (2 1/2") squares.

1 square = 1/2 bread, 1 fat exchanges
100 calories   5 grams fat
9 grams carb.   162 mg sodium
4 grams protein   25 mg cholesterol

CHERRY APPLE CRISP

Delicious any time. Other fruits may be substituted.

> 3 medium sized cooking apples, peeled and chopped
> 1 can pie cherries, packed in water
> 2 Tbsp. cornstarch
> 1/2 cup fruit sweetener
> 2 tsp. almond flavoring
> 3/4 cup flour
> 1 cup rolled oats or grape-nut type cereal
> 2 tsp. cinnamon
> 1/4 cup fruit sweetener
> 1/3 cup margarine (melted)

Place chopped apples in medium bowl. Drain cherries, saving juice. Add cherries to apples. Set aside. In small saucepan combine cherry juice, cornstarch, and fruit sweetener. Stir over medium heat until thickened. Remove from heat, add almond flavoring and pour over fruit. Pour entire fruit mixture into 9 inch square pan which has been sprayed with non-stick coating. Combine remaining ingredients, mixing to crumb-like consistency. Sprinkle over fruit combination. Bake 25-30 minutes at 325 degrees.

Makes 12 pieces.

1 piece = 1 fruit, 1 bread, 1 fat exchanges
174 calories   6 grams fat
29 grams carb.   61 mg sodium
2 grams protein   0 mg cholesterol

HEAVENLY CHOCOLATE CLOUD

This is rich and gooey! A chocolate delight.

    1 pkg. unflavored gelatin
    1/4 cup water
    3 Tbsp. fruit sweetener
    2/3 cup fruit sweetened fudge sauce
    3 egg whites
    1 tsp. cream of tartar
    2 tsp. vanilla
    1 small or 1/2 large Angel Food or Chiffon
    Cake torn in bite size pieces
    1/2 cup slivered almonds (toasted)

Dissolve gelatin in water. In top of double boiler combine fruit sweetener and gelatin. Stir over medium heat until gelatin is just dissolved. Remove from heat. Blend in fudge sauce and set aside until cool. Combine egg whites and cream of tartar and beat until whites hold stiff peaks. Add vanilla. Slowly pour chocolate mixture into egg whites and beat until blended. Into this mixture fold cake, which has been torn into walnut size pieces. Spoon into dessert dishes and top with toasted almonds. Cover and refrigerate.

Makes 16 servings.

1 serving = 1 bread, 1 fat exchanges
140 calories   5 grams fat
18 grams carb.   77 mg sodium
3 grams protein   trace of cholesterol

LEMON CUSTARD CLOUD

Tart & tangy; rich, yet light!

   3 egg yolks
   1/2 cup fresh lemon juice
   2/3 cup fruit sweetener
   2 Tbsp. cornstarch
   1/4 cup water
   1/3 cup instant mashed potato flakes
   6 egg whites
   1 tsp. cream of tartar
   1 small Angel Food or Chiffon Cake

Place egg yolks, lemon juice and fruit sweetener
in small saucepan. In small dish dissolve
cornstarch in water. Add this to lemon mixture.
Blend in potato flakes. Stir over medium heat
until mixture thickens. Cool thoroughly. Beat egg
whites and cream of tartar until stiff peaks
form. Fold in cooled lemon mixture. Tear cake
into walnut size pieces and fold into lemon
mixture. Spoon into dessert glasses or glass
square pan. Chill until ready to serve.

Makes 16 servings.

1 serving = 1 bread, 1 fat exchanges
130 calories   5 grams fat
18 grams carb.   88 mg sodium
3 grams protein   51 mg cholesterol

PINEAPPLE UPSIDE DOWN CAKE

Ronny's favorite dessert. A nice reminder of
Hawaii on a cold wintry day.

> 2 Tbsp. margarine,(melted)
> 1/4 cup fruit sweetener
> 1 cup sliced pineapple in own juice
> (approx. 1 lb. 4 oz.)
> 16 walnut or pecan halves
> 1/2 cup fruit sweetener
> 1/3 cup margarine
> 1 egg
> 2 tsp. vanilla
> 2/3 cup milk
> 1 1/2 cup flour
> 2 tsp. baking powder
> 1 tsp. salt

Combine melted margarine and 1/4 cup fruit
sweetener and spread evenly in 9 inch square or
round pan. Drain pineapple, reserving 1/4 cup of
the juice. Arrange pineapple rings in pan.
Arrange nuts around pineapple. In large bowl
combine 1/2 cup fruit sweetener and margarine.
Blend in slightly beaten egg and vanilla. Add
reserved pineapple juice and milk. In separate
bowl, combine dry ingredients and add to batter.
Pour batter over pineapple. Bake 25-35 minutes
at 350 degrees or until cake springs back when
lightly touched. Turn upside down onto serving
platter and let set a few minutes.

Makes 16 servings.

1 serving = 1 fruit, 1/2 bread, 1 1/2 fat exchanges
160 calories   7 grams fat
22 grams carb.   235 mg sodium
2 grams protein   17 mg cholesterol

SOUR CREAM RAISIN TARTS

Tasty treat for tea time or lunch boxes.

        pastry for 2-crust pie
        1 jar Fruit Mincemeat by Wax Orchards*
        1/2 cup raisins
        1/4 cup chopped nuts
        1/4 cup sour cream
        1/4 cup non-fat yogurt

Make pastry and divide dough in half. Roll out
each portion of dough into 6" square (1/8"
thick). With fluted pastry cutter, cut dough into
sixteen 4" squares. Combine Fruit Mincemeat,
raisins, nuts, sour cream, and yogurt in medium
bowl. Place spoonful of raisin filling on each
tart. Fold diagonally into triangle and seal.
Place tarts on Teflon coated cookie sheet. Bake
8-12 minutes (or until golden) at 350 degrees.

Makes 32 tarts.

1 tart = 2/3 fruit, 1 fat exchanges
82 calories   4 grams fat
10 grams carb.   33 mg sodium
1 gram protein   trace of cholesterol

* To make your own mincemeat:
      Combine: 1/2 cup fruit sweetener
             1/3 cup chopped nuts
             3/4 cup chopped apple
             2 tsp. rum flavoring

STRAWBERRY CREAM NESTS

Your friends will think you visited a Bavarian bakery!

      3 egg whites
      1 tsp. cream of tartar
      3 Tbsp. fruit sweetener
      1 tsp. vanilla

Beat egg whites and cream of tartar until thick. Slowly, add fruit sweetener and vanilla. Beat until stiff. On cookie sheet which has been covered with brown paper, make 10 mounds. With spoon make each mound into a cup-like nest, approximately 4" in diameter. Bake 45 minutes at 275 degrees. Turn off oven. Leave nests in oven one more hour or overnight. Let dry before removing from paper.

Filling:
Slice 1 1/2 cups strawberries which have been drizzled with 3 Tbsp. fruit sweetener. Spoon strawberries into nests. If desired, top with whipped cream which has been lightly sweetened with fruit sweetener (1/2 cup whipping cream (whipped)* + 1 Tbsp. fruit sweetener). Fruit sweetened, strawberry or French vanilla ice cream can also be used. Top with one whole strawberry.

Blueberries, blackberries, or peaches also work well as a substitute for strawberries.

Makes 10 nests.

1 nest = 1/2 fruit exchange
35 calories	trace of fat
7 grams carb.	15 mg sodium
1 grams protein	trace of cholesterol

* a low-fat whipped topping may be substituted.

STRAWBERRY SHORTCAKE

What's more American than summer, strawberries, and shortcake?

        4 cups fresh strawberries
        3 Tbsp. fruit sweetener
        1 1/2 cups flour
        1/2 tsp. salt
        3 tsp. baking powder
        1/2 cup instant mashed potato flakes
        1/3 cup margarine
        1 cup skim milk
        3 Tbsp. Fruit Sweet
        whipped cream (optional)

Wash, stem and slice berries. Drizzle with 3 Tbsp. fruit sweetener. Chill. Combine flour, salt, and baking powder. With fork, blend in potato flakes. Cut in margarine. Combine milk and 3 Tbsp. fruit sweetener and add to dough. Mix well. Spread dough in 8" round springform pan or 9" square pan which has been sprayed with non-stick coating. Bake 10-15 minutes at 375 degrees. Cool slightly. If using springform pan, whole cake maybe cut in half, filled with half of berries, topped with rest of cake, then remainder of berries. Serve with a dollop of whipped cream or whipped topping of your choice.

Makes 9 servings.

1 serving = 1 fruit, 1 bread, 1 1/2 fat exchanges
204 calories   7 grams fat
31 grams carb.   319 mg sodium
4 grams protein   trace of cholesterol

CHOCOLATE ICE CREAM

A chocolate lover's delight!

1 pkg. gelatin
1/4 cup water
2 cups evaporated skim milk
1/2 cup fruit sweetened fudge sauce
dash salt
1/2 cup fruit sweetener
3 cups non-fat plain yogurt
3 Tbsp. vanilla

Dissolve gelatin in water. In medium saucepan combine dissolved gelatin, milk, fudge sauce, and salt. Stir over medium heat until well blended. Stir in fruit sweetener, yogurt, and vanilla. Mix thoroughly. Cool mixture. Pour into container of your ice cream freezer and follow directions for your particular freezer.

Makes 2 quarts (16 [1/2 cup] servings).

1 serving = 1/2 skim milk, 2/3 fruit exchanges
92 calories   trace of fat
16 grams carb.   81 mg sodium
5 grams protein   2 mg cholesterol

MOCHA ICE CREAM

Follow directions for Chocolate Ice Cream, but decrease evaporated milk to 1 1/2 cups and add 1/2 cup of very strong coffee to milk. 1 cup (40 ea) toasted slivered almonds may be added after vanilla.

Makes 2 quarts (16 [1/2 cup] servings)

1 serving = 1/2 skim milk, 2/3 fruit, 1 fat exchanges
128 calories   4 grams fat
17 grams carb.   73 mg sodium
6 grams protein   2 mg cholesterol

FRENCH VANILLA ICE CREAM

If French vanilla is your flavor, then this is
for you!

    2 eggs
    1 cup fruit sweetener
    4 cups non-fat yogurt
    2 cups evaporated skim milk
    dash salt
    2 Tbsp. vanilla
    2 tsp. rum flavoring

In large bowl, beat eggs until foamy. Add fruit
sweetener. Blend in yogurt, evaporated milk,
salt, vanilla, and rum flavoring. Mix thoroughly.
Pour into container of your ice cream freezer and
follow directions for your freezer.

Makes approximately 2 quarts (16 [1/2 cup] servings)

1 serving = 3/4 skim milk, 1/2 fruit exchanges
105 calories   1 grams fat
17 grams carb.   101 mg sodium
6 grams protein   36 mg cholesterol

STRAWBERRY ICE CREAM

Great dessert for 4th of July, topped with a few blueberries.

1 pkg. plain gelatin
1/4 cup water
2 cups evaporated skim milk
1/2 cup fruit sweetener
1/4 tsp. salt
4 cups non-fat yogurt
2 Tbsp. vanilla
1 1/2 cups mashed fresh strawberries
(sweeten with fruit sweetener if desired)

Combine gelatin and water until gelatin is dissolved. In medium saucepan combine gelatin, evaporated milk, fruit sweetener, and salt. Stir over medium heat until well blended (5 minutes). Remove from heat and stir in yogurt and vanilla. Add mashed strawberries and mix well. Pour into container for your ice cream freezer and follow directions for your particular freezer. May be frozen in ice cube trays, if desired.

Makes 2 quarts (16 [1/2 cup] servings).

1 serving = 1/2 skim milk 1/2 fruit exchanges
82 calories   trace of fat
14 grams carb.   111 mg sodium
6 grams protein   2 mg cholesterol

NOTES

BREADS & BREAKFAST

© 1989

ALMOND BANANA BREAD

Tasty, healthy snack. Nice for brunch, tea, or dessert!

1/2 cup margarine
2/3 cup fruit sweetener
1 egg
2 tsp. almond extract
1 cup mashed banana
1/2 cup wheat germ
1 1/2 cups flour
1 tsp. baking powder
1 tsp. baking soda
1/4 tsp. salt
2 tsp. cinnamon
1 tsp. nutmeg
1/2 cup chopped nuts (optional)

Cream margarine and fruit sweetener. Add egg and almond flavoring. Beat well. Mix in banana. In separate bowl, combine wheat germ, flour, baking powder, baking soda, salt, cinnamon, and nutmeg. Add to batter. Stir in nuts. Pour into 9x5x3 inch loaf pan which has been sprayed with non-stick coating. Bake 35-45 minutes at 350 degrees. Bread is done when center is dry and firm.

Makes 16 slices.

1 slice = 1/2 fruit, 1 bread, 1 fat exchanges
150 calories   7 grams fat
20 grams carb.   174 mg sodium
3 grams protein   17 mg cholesterol

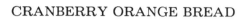

CRANBERRY ORANGE BREAD

A truer friend there cannot be than one who shares her recipe! Thank you Susan. Great at Thanksgiving!

2 cups flour
1/2 tsp. baking powder
1/2 tsp. salt
1/2 tsp. baking soda
2/3 cup fruit sweetener
1/3 cup orange juice concentrate
1/4 cup boiling water
2 Tbsp. grated orange rind
1/4 cup oil
1 egg
1 cup finely chopped cranberries*
1/2 cup chopped nuts

Combine first four ingredients and set aside. Blend fruit sweetener, orange juice concentrate, and boiling water. Stir in orange rind, oil, and egg. Beat into dry ingredients. Add cranberries and nuts. Pour into 9x5x3 inch loaf pan which has been sprayed with non-stick coating. Bake 40-50 minutes at 350 degrees.

*You can chop cranberries in blender or processor when they are frozen. Chop 2 or 3 bags of cranberries and put in freezer containers to use throughout the year.

Makes 16 slices.

1 slice = 1/2 fruit, 1 bread, 1 fat exchanges
152 calories   6 grams fat
21 grams carb.   102 mg sodium
3 grams protein   17 mg cholesterol

DATE BREAD

Moist and tasty. Especially good hot.

> 1/2 cup nuts or sunflower seeds
> 1 cup chopped dates
> 1 1/2 tsp. baking soda
> 1/2 tsp. salt
> 1/4 cup margarine
> 3/4 cup boiling water
> 2 eggs
> 2 tsp. vanilla
> 1/2 cup fruit sweetener
> 1 1/2 cups flour

Mix nuts, dates, baking soda, salt, and margarine in large bowl. Pour boiling water over these ingredients and let stand 20 minutes. Beat in eggs and vanilla. Add fruit sweetener and blend well. Stir in flour. Pour batter into 9x5x3 inch loaf pan which has been sprayed with non-stick coating. Bake 45-50 minutes at 350 degrees (or until dry and firm in center).

Makes 16 slices.

1 slice = 1 fruit, 1/2 bread, 1 fat exchanges
152 calories   6 grams fat
22 grams carb.   180 mg sodium
3 grams protein   34 mg cholesterol

LEMON BREAD

Tangy & refreshing. Nice with a summer salad.

1/2 cup margarine
2/3 cup fruit sweetener
1 egg
2 tsp. vanilla
1/2 cup lemon juice
1/4 cup non-fat yogurt
1 large lemon (grate peel; remove white; finely chop pulp)
2 1/4 cups flour
1 tsp. baking powder
1 tsp. salt
1 tsp. baking soda
1/2 cup wheat germ
1/2 cup chopped nuts

Cream margarine and fruit sweetener. Add egg and vanilla. Blend in lemon juice and yogurt. Stir in lemon peel and chopped pulp. In separate bowl, combine flour, baking powder, salt, baking soda, and wheat germ. Add to batter. Stir in nuts. Pour batter into 9x5x3 inch loaf pan which has been sprayed with non-stick coating. Bake 45-50 minutes at 350 degrees.

Makes 16 slices.

1 slice = 1/2 fruit, 1 bread, 1 fat exchanges
188 calories   8 grams fat
23 grams carb.   268 mg sodium
5 grams protein   17 mg cholesterol

ORANGE BREAD

A quick and easy treat for unexpected guests.

> 2 cups flour
> 3 tsp. baking powder
> 1 tsp. salt
> 1 cup finely chopped orange peel.(peel only of 2 oranges)
> 1/2 cup chopped walnuts
> 2/3 cup fruit sweetener
> 2 beaten eggs
> 1 cup milk
> 1/4 cup melted margarine

In large bowl combine flour, baking powder, and salt. Add nuts and peel to flour mixture. In separate bowl combine fruit sweetener, eggs, milk, and melted margarine. Add all at once to flour mixture. Stir until all flour is moistened. Pour batter into 9x5x3 inch loaf pan which has been sprayed with non-stick coating. Bake 40-50 minutes at 350 degrees. Cool and slice.

Makes 16 slices.

1 slice = 1 1/3 bread, 1 fat exchanges
148 calories   6 grams fat
19 grams carb.   235 mg sodium
4 grams protein   35 mg cholesterol

ZUCCHINI BREAD

A delightful companion to a rich cup of coffee!
Good at the end of summer when zucchini is in
great abundance.

1/3 cup unsweetened apple sauce
2/3 cup fruit sweetener
1/3 cup oil
2 eggs
1 tsp. lemon peel (grated)
1 Tbsp. lemon juice
2 cups flour
2 tsp. baking powder
1/2 tsp. salt
1/2 tsp. baking soda
1/2 tsp. nutmeg
1/2 tsp. cinnamon
1 cup grated zucchini
1/2 cup chopped nuts (optional)

Combine apple sauce, fruit sweetener, oil, eggs,
lemon peel, and lemon juice. Beat until well
blended. Combine dry ingredients separately in
large bowl. Add zucchini and nuts to dry mixture.
Add batter to dry ingredients and mix well. Pour
into 9x5x3 inch loaf pan which has been sprayed
with non-stick coating. Bake 35-45 minutes at 350
degrees. Cool before removing from pan.

Makes 16 slices.

1 slice = 1 bread, 1 fat exchanges
109 calories   5 grams fat
13 grams carb.   138 mg sodium
2 grams protein   34 mg cholesterol

GREAT BANANA MUFFINS

These are great. High fibre and good for you too!

1/2 cup non-fat yogurt
1/2 cup fruit sweetener
1/3 cup margarine, melted
1/4 cup unsweetened apple sauce
1 cup mashed banana
1 3/4 cups flour
1 1/2 tsp. baking soda
2 egg whites
1 cup rolled oats
1 cup bran cereal
1/2 cup raisins (optional)

In large bowl, blend yogurt, fruit sweetener, margarine, apple sauce, and mashed banana. Stir in flour and soda. In separate bowl, beat egg whites until stiff then fold into batter. Mix in rolled oats, cereal, and raisins. Spoon into 12 muffin cups which have been sprayed with non-stick coating. Bake 20 minutes at 350 degrees or until firm.

Makes 12 muffins.

1 muffin = 1 fruit, 1 bread, 1 fat exchanges
192 calories   6 grams fat
31 grams carb.   207 mg sodium
5 grams protein   trace of cholesterol

Note: Addition of raisins adds 17 calories and 4 grams carb. per muffin.

BLUEBERRY MUFFINS

We live near a wonderful blueberry farm and every year we enjoy many tasty blueberry desserts.

1/2 cup margarine
1/3 cup fruit sweetener
1/3 cup unsweetened apple sauce
1/2 cup non-fat yogurt
2 eggs
1 1/3 cups flour
1 tsp. baking soda
1/2 tsp. baking powder
1 tsp. salt
1 tsp. vanilla
1 1/2 cups fresh or frozen blueberries
1/2 cup chopped pecans (optional)

Cream margarine, fruit sweetener, apple sauce, and yogurt. Beat in eggs, one at a time. Combine dry ingredients separately and stir into batter. Add vanilla. Add blueberries and nuts. Spoon batter into 15 muffin cups which have been sprayed with non-stick coating. Bake 20-25 minutes at 350 degrees.

Makes 15 muffins.

1 muffin = 1 bread, 1 1/2 fat exchanges
140 calories   7 grams fat
17 grams carb.   283 mg sodium
3 grams protein   37 mg cholesterol

Note: Addition of pecans adds 24 calories and 2 grams of fat per muffin.

BRAN MUFFINS

A traditional standby. Good to eat and good for you! Thank you Debbie Lewallen for inspiring this.

1/4 cup margarine
1/2 cup fruit sweetener
1/3 cup unsweetened apple sauce
1 cup non-fat yogurt
2 egg whites
1/2 cup whole wheat flour
3/4 cup white flour
1 1/2 tsp. baking soda
2 cups nutrigrain raisin bran flakes
2 tsp. orange rind
1/2 cup sunflower seeds (optional)

Combine margarine, fruit sweetener, apple sauce, yogurt, and egg whites. Beat well. In separate bowl, combine flours and soda. Add to batter mixing well. Fold in cereal, orange rinds, and sunflower seeds. Spoon batter into 16 muffin cups which have been sprayed with a non-stick coating. Bake 15 minutes at 350 degrees. Drizzle small amount of fruit sweetener over top of each muffin if desired.

Makes 16 muffins.

1 muffin = 1 bread, 1/2 fat exchanges
107 calories   3 grams fat
17 grams carb.   152 mg sodium
3 grams protein   0 mg cholesterol

Note: Addition of seeds adds 25 calories and 2 grams of fat per muffin.

LEMON TREE MUFFINS

Tart, tangy, and tasty!

    1/2 cup margarine
    1/2 cup fruit sweetener
    1 Tbsp. grated lemon rind
    3 egg whites
    1 cup flour
    1 tsp. baking powder
    1/4 tsp. salt
Topping
    3 Tbsp. lemon juice
    2 Tbsp. fruit sweetener
    1 tsp. nutmeg
    1/4 cup chopped nuts

Cream margarine with fruit sweetener. Add lemon rind and egg whites. Beat well. Separately, blend flour, baking soda, and salt. Add to egg mixture. Spoon into 12 muffin cups sprayed with non-stick coating. Combine lemon juice, fruit sweetener, nutmeg, and nuts. Sprinkle over each muffin. Bake 15-20 minutes at 350 degrees.

Makes 12 muffins.

1 muffin = 1/2 fruit, 1/2 bread, 2 fat exchanges
160 calories   9 grams fat
17 grams carb.   135 mg sodium
3 grams protein   0 mg cholesterol

OATMEAL MUFFINS

Hearty! Great with an espresso for mid-morning!
Serve them warm with a pure, fruit sweetened,
black cherry jelly.

  1 cup rolled oats
  1 cup non-fat yogurt
  1/2 cup margarine
  2/3 cup fruit sweetener
  1/4 cup unsweetened apple sauce
  2 egg whites
  1 cup flour
  1 tsp. baking soda
  1/4 tsp. salt

Soak oats in yogurt for 30 minutes. In mixing
bowl, combine margarine, fruit sweetener, and apple
sauce. Mix well. Blend in slightly beaten egg
whites. Add oat mixture and beat well. In separate
bowl combine dry ingredients, then add to batter
until well blended. Pour into 12 muffin cups,
which have been sprayed with non-stick coating.
Bake 12-15 minutes at 350 degrees.

Makes 12 muffins.

1 muffin = 1/2 fruit, 1 bread, 1 1/2 fat exchanges
186 calories   8 grams fat
24 grams carb.   220 mg sodium
4 grams protein   0 mg cholesterol

RASPBERRY CREAM CHEESE MUFFINS

Also great with blueberries, blackberries, or
sliced strawberries.

    1 cup fresh or frozen raspberries
    2 Tbsp. fruit sweetener (or to your taste)
    1/4 cup low-fat ricotta cheese
    1/2 cup margarine
    1/2 cup fruit sweetener
    1/3 cup unsweetened apple sauce
    1/2 cup low-fat ricotta cheese
    2 egg whites
    1 1/2 cups flour
    1 1/2 tsp. baking soda
    1 tsp. salt
    1/4 cup chopped nuts (optional)

In small bowl, combine raspberries, 2 Tbsp. fruit
sweetener, and 1/4 cup ricotta cheese. Set aside.
In large bowl, cream margarine, 1/2 cup fruit
sweetener, apple sauce, and 1/2 cup ricotta
cheese. Beat in egg whites. Separately, combine
flour, baking powder, and salt. Fold dry mixture
into batter. Add nuts. Gently, fold raspberry
mixture into batter until marbled through. Spoon
batter into 15 muffin tins which have been
sprayed with non-stick coating. Bake 15-20
minutes at 350 degrees.

Makes 15 large muffins.

1 muffin = 1/2 fruit, 1 bread, 1 fat exchanges
157 calories   7 grams fat
20 grams carb.   305 mg sodium
3 grams protein   4 mg cholesterol

Note: Addition of nuts adds 10 calories and
1 gram fat per muffin.

YOGURT MUFFINS

Light and delicious! Nice for a summer brunch.

1/2 cup margarine
1/2 cup fruit sweetener
1/2 cup unsweetened apple sauce
1 egg + 2 egg whites
3/4 cup non-fat yogurt
2 1/4 cup flour
1 tsp. baking soda
1/2 tsp. salt
2 tsp. vanilla
1 cup blueberries
1/3 cup chopped nuts (optional)

Blend together first three ingredients. Beat in
egg and egg whites. Add yogurt and mix well. Blend
dry ingredients separately, then stir into batter.
Add vanilla. Fold in berries and nuts. Spoon
into 12 muffin cups which have been sprayed with
non-stick coating spray. Bake 15-20 minutes at
350 degrees.

Makes 16 muffins

1 muffin = 1/2 fruit, 1 bread, 1 fat exchanges
155 calories   6 grams fat
21 grams carb.   198 mg sodium
3 grams protein   17 mg cholesterol

Note: Addition of nuts adds 16 calories and
2 grams fat per muffin.

STUFFIN' MUFFINS

So good and filling! So good for you! A hiker's delight!

- 1 cup low-fat ricotta cheese
- 1/2 cup unsweetened apple sauce
- 1/2 cup fruit sweetener
- 2 Tbsp. oil
- 1 egg
- 2 tsp. vanilla
- 1 1/4 cups flour
- 1/2 cup wheat germ
- 1 tsp. baking soda
- 1/2 tsp. baking powder
- 1 tsp. nutmeg
- 1 tsp. allspice
- 1 cup shredded zucchini or carrots, or combination of both
- 1/4 cup chopped apple
- 1/4 cup raisins
- 1/4 cup sunflower seeds (optional)

In large bowl, cream ricotta, apple sauce, fruit sweetener, and oil. Stir in egg and vanilla. In separate bowl combine flour, wheat germ, soda, baking powder, nutmeg, and allspice. Add to batter; blend well. Add zucchini, apples, raisins, and sunflower seeds. Spoon into 15 muffin cups which have been sprayed with non-stick coating. Bake 20=25 minutes (or until firm and golden brown) at 350 degrees.

Makes 15 muffins.

1 muffin = 1 bread, 1 fat exchanges
131 calories   4 grams fat
19 grams carb.   92 mg sodium
5 grams protein   23 mg cholesterol

Note: Addition of seeds adds 7 calories per muffin.

APRICOT ALMOND COFFEE CAKE

A wonderful addition to any brunch.

1 cup water
1 cup dried apricots (cut in small pieces)
1/4 cup margarine
1/2 cup fruit sweetener
1/2 cup unsweetened apple sauce
1 egg white
1 1/2 cups flour
2 tsp. baking powder
1/2 tsp. salt
2 tsp. cinnamon
2 tsp. vanilla

TOPPING:
1/4 cup fruit sweetener
1/2 cup instant mashed potato flakes
2 Tbsp. melted margarine
1/4 cup chopped, toasted almonds (20)

In saucepan, combine apricots and water. Simmer over medium heat until thick. (15 minutes) Set aside. Cream margarine, fruit sweetener, and Apple Butter. Beat in egg white. Separately, combine dry ingredients then add this mixture to batter. Drain remaining water off apricots. Add apricots and vanilla to batter. Pour batter into 9" x 9" pan which has been sprayed with non-stick coating. Combine topping ingredients until a crunchy consistency is obtained. Sprinkle on cake. Bake cake 30-35 minutes at 325 degrees.

Serves 16.

1 serving = 1 fruit, 1/2 bread, 1 fat exchanges
160 calories   5 grams fat
26 grams carb.   159 mg sodium
2 grams protein   0 mg cholesterol

CHOCOLATE SWIRL COFFEE CAKE

A marvelous treat with morning coffee!

    2 cups biscuit mix
    2 Tbsp. fruit sweetener
    2 Tbsp. margarine (melted)
    1 egg
    3/4 cup skim milk
    1/3 cup fruit sweetened fudge sauce (warm to thin slightly)

TOPPING:
    1/3 cup shredded coconut (optional)
    1/4 cup chopped nuts
    3 Tbsp. margarine (melted)
    2 Tbsp. fruit sweetener

Combine biscuit mix, fruit sweetener, margarine, egg, and milk. Beat vigorously. Pour into 9x9 inch pan which has been sprayed with non-stick coating. Spoon fudge sauce over batter and swirl through with knife. Combine topping ingredients and sprinkle over cake. Bake 25 minutes at 350 degrees, or until cake springs back when lightly touched.

Makes 16 squares.

1 square = 1 bread, 1 1/2 fat exchanges
130 calories   7 grams fat
15 grams carb.   214 mg sodium
2 grams protein   17 mg cholesterol

Note: Addition of coconut adds 10 calories and 1 gram fat per square.

DATE COFFEE CAKE

Thank you to my friend Jude, who first told me about fruit sweetened products! Yummy!

    3/4 cup water
    1 cup dates, chopped
    1 tsp. baking soda
    1/2 cup fruit sweetener
    1/2 cup margarine
    1/2 cup mashed banana
    1/4 cup unsweetened apple sauce
    2 egg whites
    1 tsp. vanilla
    2 1/2 cups flour
    2 tsp. baking powder
    dash salt
TOPPING:
    1/2 cup shredded coconut (optional)
    1/2 cup chopped nuts
    3 Tbsp. fruit sweetener
    2 Tbsp. margarine

Combine water, dates, and baking soda. Set aside. In separate bowl, cream fruit sweetener and margarine. Mix in mashed banana and apple sauce until well blended. Beat in egg whites. Add vanilla. Sift together flour, baking powder, and salt and add to batter. Slowly, blend in date mixture. Pour batter into 9" x 13" pan which has been sprayed with non-stick coating. Combine topping ingredients and sprinkle over cake. Bake 25-30 min. at 350 deg. Cake is done if it springs back when lightly touched.

Cut into 24 servings.

1 serving = 1 fruit, 1/2 bread, 1 fat exchanges
149 calories   6 grams fat
21 grams carb.   130 mg sodium
2 grams protein   0 mg cholesterol

NANA BROSIA

A delightful tropical combination of bananas and coconut. Another great addition to breakfast or brunch.

    2 cups biscuit mix
    3 Tbsp. fruit sweetener
    2/3 cup mashed banana
    1 egg
    2 Tbsp. milk
TOPPING:
    1/2 cup shredded coconut
    1/3 cup fruit sweetener
    1/4 cup margarine (melted)
    2 Tbsp. cinnamon

Combine biscuit mix, fruit sweetener, banana, egg, and milk. Beat until well blended. Set aside. Combine topping ingredients. Reserve 1/4 cup topping. Sprinkle rest of topping into 9 inch round cake pan. Pour on half batter and spread evenly. Sprinkle batter with reserved topping and then remainder of batter. Bake 20-25 minutes at 350 degrees. While still warm, invert pan onto large plate and let set for 5 minutes. Remove pan, slice, and serve.

Makes 16 slices.

1 slice = 1/2 fruit, 1/2 bread, 1 fat exchanges
147 calories   8 grams fat
17 grams carb.   233 mg sodium
2 grams protein   17 mg cholesterol

STREUSEL COFFEE CAKE

An old favorite that's still a winner!

> 1/2 cup fruit sweetener
> 1/4 cup margarine
> 1 egg
> 1/2 cup milk
> 2 tsp. vanilla
> 1 1/2 cup flour
> 2 tsp. baking powder
> 1/2 tsp. salt

TOPPING:
> 1 Tbsp. melted butter
> 1/3 cup fruit sweetener
> 2 Tbsp. flour
> 2 Tbsp. mashed potato flakes
> 2 tsp. cinnamon
> 1/4 cup chopped nuts

Cream fruit sweetener and margarine. Beat in egg and milk. Add vanilla. Combine dry ingredients and stir into batter. Pour half of batter into 8" square pan. Sprinkle with half of topping. Add remaining batter and topping. Bake 20-30 minutes at 350 degrees.

Serves 16.

1 serving = 1 bread, 1 fat exchanges
132 calories   5 grams fat
18 grams carb.   153 mg sodium
3 grams protein   19 mg cholesterol

ALMOND PUFF STRIPS

Nice and tasty! Great for breakfast, brunch, or lunch.

    1/3 cup margarine
    1 cup water
    2 tsp. almond flavoring
    1 cup flour
    3 eggs
    3 Tbsp. fruit sweetener
    2 tsp. almond flavoring
    1/4 cup toasted slivered almonds (20)

Heat margarine and water in medium saucepan until boiling. Remove from heat and add almond flavoring and flour. Stir over low heat until it forms a ball. Remove from heat and beat in eggs, one at a time. Spread dough on Teflon baking sheet in two 12x3 inch strips. Bake 20-30 minutes (or until top is puffed and golden) at 375 degrees. Combine fruit sweetener and flavoring. Drizzle over puff strips. Sprinkle with toasted almonds. Cut each strip in 6 pieces.

Makes 12 servings

1 strip = 2/3 bread, 1 1/2 fat exchanges
126 calories   8 grams fat
11 grams carb.   76 mg sodium
3 grams protein   68 mg cholesterol

BREAKFAST PUFF BUN

Ready for something different? This is it. Only
don't plan on eating just one!

CRUST:
    1/4 cup margarine
    1 cup flour
    1 Tbsp. fruit sweetener
    3 Tbsp. water
BATTER:
    1 cup water
    1/3 cup margarine
    1 cup flour
    2 eggs + 2 egg whites
    1/2 cup fruit sweetener
    2 tsp. almond flavoring
TOPPING:
    3 Tbsp. fruit sweetener
    2 Tbsp. lemon juice

Mix crust ingredients. Spread on pizza pan in 11"
circle. Set aside. For batter: combine water and
margarine in saucepan and bring to boil. Add flour.
Stir constantly until thick. Remove from heat. Add
eggs, one at a time, stirring thoroughly after each
addition. Stir in fruit sweetener and almond flavoring.
Spread batter over crust, leaving 1" of crust
showing around edge of circle. Bake 20 minutes at
350 degrees. Cool slightly. Drizzle with topping
and with 1/4 cup toasted almonds.(20 almonds)

Makes 16 servings.

1 serving = 1 bread, 1 1/2 fat exchanges
157 calories   8 grams fat
19 grams carb.   91 mg sodium
3 grams protein   34 mg cholesterol

Note: addition of almonds adds 18 calories and
2 grams fat per serving.

BERRY FAVORITE BREAKFAST BARS

One of my favorite easy recipes! Great for a
holiday brunch treat.

        2 cups biscuit mix
        1/4 cup low-fat ricotta cheese
        1/4 cup margarine
        2 Tbsp. fruit sweetener
        1/2 cup milk
        1/4 cup unsweetened apple sauce
        1 cup mashed berries sweetened with 3 Tbsp.
        Fruit Sweet
FROSTING:
        3 Tbsp. fruit sweetener
        2 Tbsp. almond flavoring
        1 Tbsp. milk

Cut ricotta cheese and margarine into biscuit
mix. Blend in fruit sweetener and milk. Knead on
floured surface. Roll into 14x9 inch rectangle.
Turn onto Teflon coated cookie sheet. Spread
apple sauce down center 1/3 of dough. Cover this
area with sweetened berries. Make 3" cuts at 1"
intervals on each side. Fold strips over filling
for braid effect. Bake 15-20 minutes at 400
degrees. Combine frosting ingredients and drizzle
over braid.

Makes 16 bars.

1 bar = 1 bread, 1 fat exchanges
116 calories   5 grams fat
16 grams carb.   205 mg sodium
2 grams protein   trace of cholesterol

NOTES

SIPS 'N SNACKS

© 1989 PL

ORANGE JULIE

1/3 cup orange juice concentrate
1/2 cup cold water
1/2 cup cold milk
2 Tbsp. fruit sweetener
1 tsp. vanilla

Place all ingredients in blender. Add 6 ice cubes and blend for 30 seconds. Pour into chilled glasses.

Makes 3 servings.

1 serving = 1 fruit exchange
82 calories   0 grams fat
18 grams carb.   21 mg sodium
2 grams protein   0 mg cholesterol

ORANGE FROST

1 can mandarin oranges, water packed
2 bananas
1/4 cup non-fat yogurt
1-12 oz. can orange juice concentrate
3 Tbsp. fruit sweetener

Combine all ingredients in blender. Add 8 ice cubes and blend for 60 seconds. Pour into punch bowl and add 2 quarts soda water.

Makes 24 (1/2 cup) servings.

1 serving = 2/3 fruit exchange
47 calories   trace of fat
11 grams carb.   2 mg sodium
1 grams protein   trace of cholesterol

BANANA SLUSH

In blender combine:

    3 ripe bananas (sliced or chunk)
    1-12 oz. can frozen pineapple juice
    concentrate, unsweetened
    1-12 oz. can orange juice concentrate
    1/2 cup lemon juice

Blend 30 seconds. Pour into punch bowl. Add 2-3
quarts soda water. The basic blend may be made
ahead and frozen. Thaw 2 hours and then add soda.

Makes 24 (1/2 cup) servings.

1 serving = 1 fruit exchange
70 calories   trace of fat
17 grams carb.   2 mg sodium
1 grams protein   0 mg cholesterol

EVERGREEN PUNCH

    1/2 cup lemon juice
    1/2 cup lime juice
    1-12 oz. can frozen apple juice

Mix together in punch bowl. Pour 2 quarts lemon
flavored seltzer or soda water over juices. Top
with 4 cups crushed ice.

Makes 18 (1/2 cup) servings.

1 serving = 2/3 fruit exchange
40 calories   0 grams fat
10 grams carb.   6 mg sodium
trace of protein   0 mg cholesterol

ESKIMO DELIGHT

    1 1/2 cups chilled strong coffee
    3 Tbsp. fruit sweetened fudge sauce
    1 1/2 cups cold skim milk
    1/2 cup crushed ice
    1 tsp. vanilla or vanilla powder

Combine all ingredients in blender. Beat until
smooth. Pour in tall glasses and top with a dollop
of whipped cream, if desired. Sprinkle with cinnamon.

Serves 3, each cup = 2/3 fruit, 1 skim milk exchange
95 calories   trace of fat
16 grams carb.   67 mg sodium
4 grams protein   2 mg cholesterol

ONA ONA MOCHA

A take off of a treat from our Hawaii days!

    1 cup chilled coffee
    1 1/2 cups milk
    1 cup crushed ice
    1 cup French Vanilla Ice Cream (see recipe)
        (optional)
    3 Tbsp. fruit sweetened fudge sauce
    3 Tbsp. peanut butter

Combine all ingredients in blender and blend for
1 minute. Pour in tall glasses and sprinkle with
powdered vanilla or cocoa. (for an extra treat,
blend in a banana)

Serves 4, each cup = 1 fruit, 1/2 skim milk, 1 fat ex.
168 calories   6 grams fat
21 grams carb.   105 mg sodium
7 grams protein   trace of cholesterol

Note: with addition of banana ice cream, 1 serving =
1 fruit, 1 skim milk, 2 fat exchanges

CITRUS CREME PUNCH

10-12 ice cubes
1-16 oz. can frozen orange juice concentrate
1/4 cup fruit sweetener
2 Tbsp. vanilla
2 qt. soda water

In blender, combine juice concentrate, fruit
sweetener, vanilla and ice cubes. Blend 30
seconds. Pour into punch bowl. Add additional ice
if desired. Pour soda water over orange juice.
Garnish with orange slices.

Serves 10, each 1 cup serving = 1 1/2 fruit exchanges
105 calories   0 grams fat
25 grams carb.   2 mg sodium
1 grams protein   0 mg cholesterol

GINGER FIZZ

2 tsp. ginger
3 Tbsp. fruit sweetener
2-12 oz. cans frozen sugar-free apple juice
1/2 cup lemon juice
3 qt. soda water

Combine first four ingredients in punch bowl. Mix
well. Add soda water. Garnish with ice ring and
mint leaves.

Serves 14, each 1 cup serving = 1 1/2 fruit exchanges
105 calories   trace of fat
26 grams carb.   14 mg sodium
trace protein   0 mg cholesterol

TRUFFLES

These are heavenly! In fact, they go so fast you may not need to store them.

> 1/2 cup fruit sweetened fudge sauce
> 1/2 cup instant mashed potato flakes
> 3 Tbsp. finely ground almonds
> 2 Tbsp. almond flavoring or Amaretto

In medium bowl combine ingredients and cream until smooth. Roll into walnut size balls. Into a 1/2 cup of finely ground almonds, roll each truffle. Chill. For variation other flavors such as Grand Marnier, Kahlua, or rum maybe substituted for Amaretto. Store Truffles in tightly covered plastic storage container.

Makes 16.

1 Truffle = 1/2 fruit exchange
40 calories	trace of fat
7 grams carb.	2 mg sodium
trace protein	0 mg cholesterol

MOMONA CHEESE BALLS

A sinfully rich tasting treat without the calories!

  3 Tbsp. fruit sweetener
  1/2 cup low-fat Neufchatel
  1/2 cup low-fat ricotta cheese
  2/3 cup (or 40 nuts) chopped, blanched almonds
  1 cup shredded coconut

Cream together fruit sweetener, low-fat Neufchatel cheese, and ricotta. Add nuts. Blend well. Roll into 1" balls. Roll each ball in 1 cup coconut and store in sealed plastic container. Chill.

Makes 30 cookies.

1 ball = 1 fat exchanges
52 calories   4 grams fat
3 grams carb.   28 mg sodium
2 grams protein 4 mg cholesterol

4 balls = 1 skim milk, 3 fat exchanges
208 calories   16 grams fat
12 grams carb. 112 mg sodium
8 grams protein 12 mg cholesterol

KRISPIE KUBES

Crispy, crunchy, and light!

   1/2 cup fruit sweetener
   1/2 cup peanut butter
   1/2 cup instant mashed potato flakes
   2 tsp. vanilla
   3 cups crispy rice cereal

In a large bowl, combine fruit sweetener and
peanut butter. Micro-wave on high from 1-2
minutes. Add mashed potato flakes and vanilla.
Cool slightly. Stir in rice cereal. Press into
9 x 9" Teflon coated pan. Refrigerate for two
hours. When cool, cut into squares.

Makes 20 bars.

1 bar = 2/3 fruit, 1/2 fat exchanges
75 calories   3 grams fat
10 grams carb.   82 mg sodium
2 grams protein   0 mg cholesterol

NOTES

NOTES

ORANGE CREAM TOPPING

Good and light. Nice topping for Gingerbread!

        2 Tbsp. cornstarch
        1/4 cup cold water
        1/4 cup orange juice concentrate
        1/4 cup non-fat yogurt
        1/4 cup fruit sweetener
        2 tsp. vanilla
        2 tsp. grated orange rind (optional)

Combine cornstarch and water in small sauce
pan. Blend in orange juice concentrate, yogurt
and fruit sweetener. Stir over medium heat until
thick. Remove from heat and stir in vanilla.
Serve hot or store in refrigerator.

Makes 1 cup.

1 cup =
340 calories   trace of fat
77 grams carb.   45 mg sodium
5 grams protein   4 mg cholesterol

3 Tbsp. = 1 fruit exchange
68 calories   trace of fat
16 grams carb.   9 mg sodium
1 grams protein   1 mg cholesterol

BERRY SAUCE

A marvelous way to top ice cream, pudding, or other desserts!

> 1/2 cup cold water
> 3 Tbsp. cornstarch
> 1/2 cup fruit sweetener
> 2 1/4 cups blueberries, blackberries, or raspberries
> dash salt
> 2 tsp. almond flavoring

Blend cornstarch and water in saucepan. Add fruit sweetener, 1 cup of fruit, and dash of salt. Cook over medium heat, stirring constantly, until thickened. Stir in remaining fruit and almond flavoring. Serve hot over ice cream or other dessert.

Makes approximately 2 cups fruit sauce

2 cups =
583 calories	1 grams fat
140 grams carb.	215 mg sodium
2 grams protein	0 mg cholesterol

1/4 cup serving = 1 fruit exchange
73 calories	0 grams fat
18 grams carb.	27 mg sodium
trace protein	0 mg cholesterol

GRANOLA

Crunchy and nutritious! Great for skiers and joggers as a high energy food.

    4 cups oats
    2/3 cup raisins
    2/3 cup chopped nuts
    1/2 cup fruit sweetener
    1/2 cup peanut butter

In 9x13 inch pan, which has been sprayed with non-stick coating spray, spread 4 cups rolled oats. Bake at 325 degrees for 15-20 minutes until golden brown. Stir mixture once or twice while browning. Remove oats from oven. Add raisins and nuts.

In small saucepan combine the fruit sweetener and peanut butter. Heat just until mixture becomes liquid. Pour syrup over oat mixture and mix until all oats are moistened. Return mixture to oven for 15-20 minutes. Cool mixture well, then store in covered container. Serve as cereal with milk, or top with fruit or non-fat yogurt.

Makes 18 (1/3 cup) servings.

1 serving = 1 1/2 bread, 1 1/2 fat exchanges
172 calories   7 grams fat
22 grams carb.   35 mg sodium
6 grams protein   0 mg cholesterol

WHIPPED TOPPING

Great replacement for whipping cream.

    2 egg whites
    2 Tbsp. fruit sweetener
    1-2 tsp. vanilla or other flavoring

Beat egg whites until fluffy. Slowly add fruit sweetener, and beat until mixture peaks. Add vanilla. Great topping for pudding, Dutch Apple Cake, Fruit Pie.

For whole recipe:
110 calories   0 grams fat
19 grams carb.   100 mg sodium
7 grams protein   0 mg cholesterol

1 serving (1/4 of recipe) = 1/3 fruit exchange
28 calories   0 grams fat
5 grams carb.   25 mg sodium
2 grams protein   0 mg cholesterol

NUTRITIONAL CHART*

FOOD	AMOUNT	KCAL Kc	CARB Gm	PROT Gm	FAT Gm	SOD Mg
almonds	1 cup	766	26	25	67	14
apple, raw	1	81	21	0	0	1
apple juice frz	1 cup	111	27	0	0	17
apple sauce	1 cup	106	27	0	0	0
apricots	.5 cup	155	40	2	0	6
baking soda	1 tsp.	0	0	0	0	821
banana, raw	1	105	26	1	0	1
berries (straw)	1 cup	45	10	0	0	2
biscuit mix	1 cup	424	68	7	12	1300
bran cereal	1 cup	127	30	4	0	363
buttermilk	1 cup	99	11	8	2	257
cherries, sour	1 cup	87	21	1	0	17
chocolate	1 oz.	146	8	3	15	1
chocolate chips	1 cup	770	125	6	35	63
coconut, dried	1 cup	466	44	2	33	244
corn flakes	1 cup	88	19	1	0	281
corn starch	1 Tbsp.	28	7	0	0	0
cottage cheese	1 cup	203	8	31	4	918
dates, dried	1 cup	489	131	3	0	5
egg	1	79	0	6	5	69
egg yolk	1	63	0	2	5	8
egg white	1	16	0	3	0	50
evap. sk milk	1 cup	199	28	19	0	293
flour, wheat	1 cup	455	95	13	1	2
fruit sweetener	1 Tbsp.	39	9	0	0	-
fruit sweetened fudge topping	1 Tbsp.	48	9	-	-	-
graham crackers	1 7 grms	27	5	0	0	33
margarine	.5 cup	808	1	1	90	1056
mayonnaise	1 Tbsp.	98	0	0	11	78
milk	1 cup	86	11	8	0	126

NUTRITIONAL CHART (continued)

FOOD	AMOUNT	KCAL Kc	CARB Gm	PROT Gm	FAT Gm	SOD Mg
Neufchatel	2 oz.	149	1	5	13	228
oatmeal	1 cup	311	54	13	5	3
oil	1 Tbsp.	120	0	0	13	0
orange, raw	1	62	15	1	0	0
orange juice frz	1 cup	112	26	1	0	2
peanut butter	1 Tbsp.	95	2	4	8	75
pineapple juice	1 cup	150	39	1	0	4
potato flk.	.5 cup	101	23	2	0	24
pumpkin	1 cup	83	19	2	0	12
raisins	.5 cup	217	57	2	0	8
rice crispies	1 cup	112	24	1	0	340
ricotta	1 cup	340	12	28	19	307
salt	1 tsp.	0	0	0	0	1955
sour cream	.5 cup	246	4	3	24	61
walnuts	1 cup	759	15	30	70	2
yogurt	1 cup	127	17	13	0	174
zucchinii	1 cup	19	3	1	0	3

* These exchanges are based on the "*1989 Revised ADA Exchange List For Meal Planning*"

INDEX

A GIFT FROM WAX ORCHARDS - RECIPE FILES

ORANGE MINCE COOKIES

　　1 egg, beaten well
　　1/2 cup vegetable oil
　　1/2 cup fruit sweetener
　　1 cup Fruit Mincemeat
　　1/2 tsp. orange flavoring
　　1 1/2 cup flour
　　1/2 tsp. baking soda
　　1/2 cup oatmeal
　　1/2 cup chopped walnuts (optional)

Blend egg, oil, fruit sweetener, Mincemeat, and flavoring.
Sift dry ingredients, add walnuts, then add to mincemeat
mix and blend. Arrange with a teaspoon on oiled cookie
sheets and bake at 350 degrees until light brown, about
8 to 12 minutes. Makes 60 cookies

Exchange: 2 cookies = 1/2 starch, 2 fat
Calories 170

RASPBERRY MOUSSE

　　2/3 cup Raspberry Fanciful
　　2 egg whites
　　1/8 tsp. cream of tartar
　　1/2 cup whipping cream

Add cream of tartar to egg whites, beat until stiff
but not dry. Fold into Raspberry Fanciful. Fold
whipped cream into fruit mixture. Chill before serving,
or freeze for frozen mousse. Makes 8 servings
Use any of the Fanciful flavors for variation.

Exchange: 1 serving = 1/2 fruit, 1 fat
Calories: 77

Diabetic Food Exchanges for Wax Orchards recipes courtesy:

Nancy Cooper, R.D., CDE, Diabetes Nutrition Specialist
International Diabetes Center - Minneapolis MN 55416

FUDGE SWEET BROWNIES

      2/3 cups flour
      1/2 tsp. baking powder
      1 egg, beaten well
      3 egg whites, whipped
      1/2 cup vegetable oil
      2/3 cups fruit sweetened fudge topping, softened
      1/2 cup fruit sweetener
      1 tsp. real vanilla
      1/2 cup chopped walnuts

Sift flour and baking powder. Set aside. Blend oil,
fruit sweetened fudge topping, fruit sweetener, and
vanilla. Add flour mixture and walnuts and blend
thoroughly. Fold in egg whites. Pour mixture into a greased
and floured 9" baking pan. Bake at 350 degrees for about 20
minutes until cake springs back at light touch.

brownie = 1 1/2 fruit, 1 starch, 1/4 meat, 3 fat exchanges
420 calories

FUDGE CRUNCH - In a Bag

      1/2 cup fruit sweetened fudge topping
      1/2 cup Peanut Butter (smooth or chunky)
      3/4 cup grape nuts
      2 Tbsp. powdered milk (non-instant)

This can be unbelievably messy, so use a bread sized plastic
bag. Put the fruit sweetened fudge topping and peanut butter
in the bag and moosh together. Add grape nuts and powdered
milk and knead in the bag. When the mixture is too dry
or too moist, adjust with fruit sweetened fudge topping or
grape nuts. Roll or knead to 1/4 " thick (in the bag). Chill in
freezer. Best in 24 hours, when grape nuts soften a bit,
or use fresh for a very crunchy candy. Cut into squares.

30 servings (1 Tbsp ea) 1 serving = 1/2 bread exchange
49 calories   2 grams fat
6 grams carb.   41 mg sodium
2 grams protein   0 cholesterol

TORTE AU CHOCOLAT

    1 3/4 cup cake flour, sifted
    3 tsp. baking powder
    1/4 tsp. salt
    1/2 tsp. cinnamon
    4 eggs, separated
    1/2 cup oil
    3/4 cup fruit sweetener
    3/4 cup fruit sweetened fudge topping
    1/2 cup milk
    1 tsp. real vanilla

Sift dry ingredients together and set aside. Combine the oil, fruit sweetener, fruit sweetened fudge topping and vanilla. Add the egg yolks to the liquid mixture, blending one at a time. Add the flour mixture to the liquid alternately with the milk. Whip the egg whites to stiff peaks and fold in gently but thoroughly.

Bake at 350 for 1/2 hour in two 9" round greased and floured tins. Cake will spring back when lightly touched. For a drier cake, bake until cake draws away from the edge of the pan. Cool.

FLUFFY FROSTING

    1 egg white, chilled
    1/4 tsp. cream of tartar
    1/2 cup Fruit Sweet
    2 tsp. real vanilla

Blend the egg white and cream of tartar together. Bring the Fruit Sweet to a boil in a small saucepan. Pour the hot syrup into the egg mixture, beating vigorously. Continue beating for several minutes until the frosting is stiff. Add vanilla. The surprising result is like 7 minute frosting.

NOTES

SWEET INSPIRATIONS ORDER FROM:

Sweet Inspirations Cookbook $12.95 each _____
Gourmet Inspirations Cookbook $12.95 each _____
Shipping / handling ($2.00 per book)   _____
Total ....

Mail Check or Money Order to:
      SWEET INSPIRATIONS INC.
      1420 NW GILMAN BLVD. #2258
      ISSAQUAH, WA. 98027

Name _____
Address _____
City _____ State _____ Zip _____

Note: Washington residents, please add 8.2% sales tax. ($1.06)

PLEASE ALLOW 4-6 WEEKS FOR DELIVERY

NOTES

NOTES

NOTES

NOTES

NOTES